Why Does Your Name Matter?

Naming, Identity, and an Invitation

William H Thompson

WESTBOW
PRESS®
A DIVISION OF THOMAS NELSON
& ZONDERVAN

Copyright © 2023 William H Thompson.

All rights reserved. No part of this book may be used or reproduced by any means, graphic, electronic, or mechanical, including photocopying, recording, taping or by any information storage retrieval system without the written permission of the author except in the case of brief quotations embodied in critical articles and reviews.

This book is a work of non-fiction. Unless otherwise noted, the author and the publisher make no explicit guarantees as to the accuracy of the information contained in this book and in some cases, names of people and places have been altered to protect their privacy.

WestBow Press books may be ordered through booksellers or by contacting:

WestBow Press
A Division of Thomas Nelson & Zondervan
1663 Liberty Drive
Bloomington, IN 47403
www.westbowpress.com
844-714-3454

Because of the dynamic nature of the Internet, any web addresses or links contained in this book may have changed since publication and may no longer be valid. The views expressed in this work are solely those of the author and do not necessarily reflect the views of the publisher, and the publisher hereby disclaims any responsibility for them.

Scripture quotations marked NASB are taken from the New American Standard Bible®, Copyright © 1960, 1962, 1963, 1968, 1971, 1972, 1973, 1975, 1977, 1995 by The Lockman Foundation. Used by permission.

Scripture quotations marked NIV are taken from the Holy Bible, New International Version®, NIV®. Copyright © 1973, 1978, 1984 by Biblica, Inc.™ Used by permission of Zondervan. All rights reserved worldwide.

The writings of Mother Teresa of Calcutta © by the Mother Teresa Center, exclusive licensee throughout the world of the Missionaries of Charity for the works of Mother Teresa. Used with permission.

ISBN: 978-1-9736-9973-6 (sc)
ISBN: 978-1-9736-9975-0 (hc)
ISBN: 978-1-9736-9974-3 (e)

Library of Congress Control Number: 2023909847

Print information available on the last page.

WestBow Press rev. date: 06/13/2023

CONTENTS

Acknowledgements vii

Foreword..xi

Introduction..xiii

1 Knowing Me 1
   - Why do I matter? Know thyself
   - A name is an introduction and an invitation

2 Knowing You 9
   - Why do you matter to me? Communication – key to knowing others
   - Words as the basis of connection with others

3 Knowing Things..20
   - Why do things matter? Naming through relationship not power
   - The difference between a word and a name

Introduction to Part Two 35

4 To Research a Name..37
   - Why do names matter?
   - Where do names come from, their journey
   - How you can use and understand them better

5 To Receive a Name..67
   - Why did your name matter to your namer?
   - A name is more than a collection of letters
   - How a name positions you in time

6 To Receive Another 81
- Why do names matter to every culture?
- The enrichment of exploring cultural naming practices
- Interviews with people from around the world

Introduction to Part Three 103

7 To Change a Name... 111
- Why does changing your name matter?
- Reasons behind a change of name
- Variation in how this change can be received

8 To Give a Name 132
- Why does the name you give matter?
- The responsibility of giving a name

9 To Be a Name... 145
- Does your name matter?
- A name as a mystery
- A name as a doorway to reconciliation and identity

References 157

ACKNOWLEDGEMENTS

I'd like to thank family and friends who have encouraged me to keep going: we aren't expected to build on our own.

Thanks to Maria Isakova Bennett and Dave Ward at the Writing Advice desk (Windows Project, Liverpool), for feedback on an early draft of this work.

My editor Theodore Brun, whose character and background made him the only person I could trust to see, understand and help me articulate the project.

My copy-editor Sarah Giles – I didn't know how much I needed you until you did what you did, thank you for pushing me towards excellence.

Rudi Palmieri, Philip Thompson, Riaan Sinden – brothers who challenged and inspire me.

All the interviewees, who gave me their time to study their experiences and freedom to share them.

My wife, Annika; thank you for supporting me through this project, and for all the reading and changes you made… you are a gift.

To Dan

FOREWORD

The more uniform the world gets, the more we seem to value our distinctives.

Most of us don't just want to blend in or go unnoticed. There is something inside us which says there is more to us than that. We want to know our unique identity, our meaning, our significant place in this ever-changing world. Whilst many of us may look to our family tree, culture, heritage, or perhaps our vocation, hobbies, interests, (or even our sports team!) to discover the answer to these deep longings, William encourages us to consider something even more fundamental. He urges us to go right back to the very beginning… our name.

William takes us on the very same journey he has been on in discovering that names truly matter. Through his intensive research and numerous interviews of people around the world, he reveals how names provide insight into our history, the hopes and dreams of those who bore us, the intrinsic value and worth we each hold and the unique character and attributes that set us apart from the other 8 billion people on the planet. Yes, you are about to discover what really *is* in a name!

So, sit back and enjoy the journey you're about to embark upon as you read this book. A journey that will help you live out your unique, distinctive story and enable you to help others as they seek to do the same.

Colin and Melissa Piper
World Evangelical Alliance

INTRODUCTION

Few things move me more like seeing joy in people's faces: that glimpse you get when you see someone change. Some of these glimpses last only moments, others a lifetime; it's like the person seems able to breathe more deeply than before.

The dinner party had moved on from the champagne and canapés when I got chatting with Graeme, the man I'd seen moving confidently amongst other guests. I'd been struck by his grace and the way that others seemed to be more alive having been with him. His eye contact during the handshake was engaging and the questions he asked me had been crafted to move beyond small talk. As in all the best dances, I took my opportunity to lead at the right moment.

'Do you know what Graeme means?' I asked him.

'No, but it was the name of my father's best friend.'

'He must have meant a lot to your father.'

'Actually, he had been a huge support to him when his father died.'

'Fascinating.'

'In what sense?'

'I love hearing about where names come from and how they give us insights into family.'

'Please, go on, William.'

'Your name and its giving suggest that your father treasures relationships...'

– he encouraged me to continue –

'...and it tells me a lot about your mum, that she understood the value of supporting your father in honouring relationships. It makes sense now why you are clearly gifted in making people feel comfortable and valued; I've seen this gift as I've watched you with people this evening.'

And there it was, washing across his face: the moment where he felt seen. The initial mystification at the personal provocation had evolved into clarity and gratitude.

We discovered that the name 'Graeme' was linked to a sense of homeliness and security which seemed to fit him well and we parted having both been moved.

What compels me towards this type of conversation? Why do I feel motivated to prompt questions and stimulate thinking? Because I think many of us sleepwalk through life and sometimes we need something to happen, or someone to say something, to jolt us into a deeper engagement with our reality. You wouldn't have picked up this book if you weren't curious. I'm glad you are and I'm keen to get started!

Writing this book has convinced me of the importance of people's names. Not only for us as individuals as we carry them, but in the way that they reveal clues about our identity, the opportunity for others to know us and the glue to restore or strengthen intergenerational relationships. It has helped me understand the importance of my own name and the value of honouring other's names. I believe that as you process the questions this book asks, it will enrich your life and the lives of those you know and meet.

There is real value in listening to how people introduce themselves. A case in point occurred this weekend. My cousin introduced me to a friend of hers: 'William, this is Dave.' 'Nice to meet you,' I said to the man being presented. 'I'm David,' he said to me with a smile. This was not said as a rebuke to my cousin, I'm not sure she even heard, but more of a clarification for me. Because I was listening, I heard. It's so easy to adapt someone's name if you think that a name is just an arbitrary collection of letters; but then maybe that's why you forget them. They're not.

A name is simple, but to look beyond the letters is complex, so in order to ensure we track together, I have had to build carefully. Thus, I have split the book into three parts.

Part One explores the significance of names and words in general – a name matters because words matter. Words can bring life and words can bring death, in different senses.

Part Two takes us deeper into the meaning and use of names, how one could draw meaning from a name and how different cultures experience the process of naming.

Part Three explores the interwoven dance between the name, the named, the namer and ultimately the maker, connecting the giving and receiving of a name with identity.

Right from the start it will be clear that I believe in an intentionality behind things. Living life is a responsibility and a decision. Life can happen to you, or you can live it. I remember a key phrase banded about at university that captures this perfectly: 'Only dead fish go with the flow.'

This isn't a 'how to' book, but a 'why?' book. Delving into names isn't a magic trick or a new method of coaching, it's simply connecting better, and if there's one thing we need, it's to connect better, to reconcile as well as 'concile'.

My sincere heart behind this book is reconciliation. Conciliation comes from the Latin *conciliare*, which means 'to bring together' and so *re*conciliation is 'to restore to union and friendship after estrangement or variance'.[1] This is what I believe names do and are for.

Maybe the person who named you asserts that it was given to you without any deliberate process – but dig a little deeper. There is always a 'yes' that took place, an often unexplainable decision that was made, the results of which you then carry. Let's explore that. Maybe you have even given a name and suddenly that name is different every time you hear it. It's connected to a part of you. Have you shared the 'why' behind it with the one you named?

***

Allow me to develop context through my own journey with my name. Imagine this scene from my childhood. My eyes focused and unfocused on the speckled grey walls of the toilet cubicle. My nose reacted to the stinging scent of bleach. My ears tracked the movements of the other schoolboys. I could hear and feel my blood coursing and my heart thumping as I tried to calm myself after another flight from them. Although my lungs were screaming for air, I forced myself to take quiet, shallow breaths so that I could hear floorboards creak, urgent whispering, a doorknob turning –anything to alert myself to an assailant's approach. This bleak sanctuary was reviling yet embracing.

'Willy' was the bullies' favourite taunt. As a teenager, I couldn't understand why my parents had named me after a body part. I reluctantly accepted being 'Skinny', or having 'Four eyes', but why hadn't my parents thought more about my name?

I have grown to love my name, but this early wrestling with it flowed out of pain – often the tool that shapes us most effectively.

I wrestled with my name as I grew up; I didn't like it as it felt like it didn't fit. Through my life I have been called Willy, Bill, Will; I even contemplated introducing myself as Liam at one point. My younger brother Philip shortened his name to Phil at school, which I liked – it seemed easy and cool – so in turn I started introducing myself as 'Will'. While repeating my A levels at a college that Phil had already attended, our mum attended an event at our youth club. Mum came home upset; I remember her telling my dad that she had overheard a parent talking about us: 'Will and Phil, fancy naming your children that, it's like Bill and Ben!' It obviously upset my mum who at the time of naming my brother probably hadn't considered the implications of future abbreviations, certainly not in light of television programmes. (Bill and Ben were children's TV characters in the 1950s.)

Nevertheless, we went our separate ways. I went to Chester and Phil went to London, reducing the possibility of awkward nomenclatural incidents. I stuck with Will which seemed to be well received. I had settled the debate in my mind: William was just too many syllables and too 'posh' sounding. Plus, the possibility of it being shortened to 'Willy' loomed large in my mind and I had no intentions of revisiting those horrors.

***

Why Does Your Name Matter?

Have you ever felt that you had the seed of an idea planted in your mind but weren't sure what to do with it? The seed for this book was planted while I volunteered in Tanzania in 1995. I spent six weeks with street children, listening to them, seeing life through their eyes as they picked their way through rubbish dumps, and training the ones who were old enough to lead. The Tanzanian people inspired me, opened my eyes, taught me, and shook my worldview.

One thing that amazed me was that people were called names such as 'Obedience' or 'Mercy,' and those with traditional names would translate them for me. For example, 'I am Ayubu, which means "patience"'. It intrigued me that they had been named so deliberately. Their names described their nature and if certain individuals assumed that I would not understand the meaning behind their names, they seemed compelled to explain them to me.

Years later I went to Hong Kong, where my hosts called me Wye Lim. They told me the Chinese characters for this name mean 'aggressively strong' and 'pure minded'. Their interpretation of my name surprised me, as neither of these characteristics would have been ones that I would have claimed if asked. Further delving when I got home revealed that 'William' was of Germanic origin, first introduced to England by William the Conqueror. It is a compound of two words: 'wil' meaning 'will or desire' and 'helm' meaning 'helmet, protection, also of the mind'. The overlap of these meanings resonated with a deep sense of who I am.

The next step was during a period of brokenness in my life. I was confronting who I was in every way and started to introduce myself as William instead of Will. This change was particularly hard for people who had known me as 'Will' for many years, but they recognised that it mattered to me. I couldn't remember mum and dad talking to me about why they had given me the name William. Henry was obvious – it was my grandpa's name – but William? Maybe they had deliberately chosen to give me a name that would have led me to having to experience and overcome adversity; Johnny Cash wrote about this in his song 'A Boy Named Sue'. The revelation of the significance of the name only came to Sue as he was about to kill the namer for what he had considered to be an abuse. Children named in this way go one of three ways: they are either crushed by it, they own it, or they change it, but I knew that my parents must have had a different reason for giving me my name. It was then that the last piece of the puzzle connected me with my first name.

I asked them what had been in their heart when they had given me my name. It turns out that I had been named after my mum's stepfather (whom I had never known). Mum said that it was to honour him for the way that he loved her as his own child. Thinking about this helped me recognise that a fundamental part of my identity was rooted in my parents and their journeys, and it resonated when I considered my own children, the first of whom is adopted. Suddenly, there was a new sense of peace, a reconciliation with this part of my identity. All the bullying was suddenly worth it: My parents had given me this name for a reason I could identify with. If this book can bring you to a point of reconciliation with yourself, your name, or your namer, it will have been a success.

Now I connect with people in a deeper way than I used to. Finding out someone's name used to be a polite box-ticking exercise, 'Hi, I am William. What's your name?' Once they had told me their name, we could move on, either to the good stuff, or to the search for a polite way to excuse myself. I'm sure that you have experienced conversations where you realise that you instantly forgot their name, and how awful that feels. Zsa Zsa Gabor got out of this with an alternative strategy; apparently she said that she called everyone 'Darling' because she couldn't remember their names. People's names actually matter to me now, it isn't just a collection of letters and a label, it's a door that I can choose to walk past or open. By paying attention to this one word, people find me more attentive and often comment on what a good listener I am. Right from the beginning of our engagement, I am building trust.

Can you see yourself reconnecting with your namer, not just by asking them why they gave you your name, but by determining yourself to see the process through their eyes?

***

Why Does Your Name Matter?

Everyone has a story and I wonder how you will explore yours as you make your way through these chapters. I have spoken to hundreds of individuals during the process of authoring this book and everyone has a unique and valuable reflection. We all share the experience of a name, whether it's to do with our given or family name, the disruption of a name through the breakdown of a family, the process of naming a child, or cherishing the name of a loved one.

A few pointers: I use the term 'namer' rather than parent or parents. Research and interviews have shown me that there are many different people who may have a part to play in naming, so I use this term to cover all of these. If the occasional academic insight stirs you, the books and academic papers are referenced at the back. Sociology, psychology, and the fabulous field of onomastics (the study of the origin, history, and use of proper names)[2] really are a Wild West horizon waiting to be ridden into.

***

The interview I conducted with Angie and Dan, that this next part draws from, is sacred for me; because you'll hear the heart of a young woman who died shortly after sharing it. Not only that, but I had known Angie since she was a child and through her teenage years as her youth worker. For me what you are about to read encapsulates one of the golden threads of this book – that your name connects you with the heart of your namer.

Angie had loved the name Theodore since she was really young. Despite not being sure if she ever wanted children, Theo/Theodore was the name she had imagined giving her son even though at the time she hadn't known what it meant.

As a young couple, she and Dan had tried for a baby for about eight years and had been through IVF. At one point they were pregnant with twins, but had lost them within the first couple of weeks. The process had been so painful that they didn't want to try again.

They were praying that it would happen naturally even though the doctors were saying that it was impossible. While away together a year after the IVF, Angie realised that she must have been pregnant and lost another baby. Further tests indicated that she was pregnant, but thinking the tests were detecting hormones from the previous pregnancy, these were discounted. But time went on and it was confirmed: they were pregnant! As far as they were concerned, Theo had been a complete miracle; he had he been conceived naturally.

They talked about a lot of names, and Angie kept reiterating that she would love to call him Theodore, as she felt she was carrying a boy. Dan came round to the idea, and they started calling him Theodore as they talked to him while he was still inside her womb. Together they finally looked up what the name meant and saw that it meant 'God's gift'. This confirmed it for them; they believed that they'd been given a gift from God.

Angie experienced significant health problems during the pregnancy – her platelets and blood cells were low and getting lower, a sign of leukaemia. All the way through the pregnancy the advice was to abort the baby, but Angie would hear none of it. The medical staff were worried about her surviving, but she told them that she would rather die trying than have anything like that happen. They realised Angie was determined and stopped mentioning it. Looking back, she was relieved that she hadn't listened. She told me that him having the name Theodore had given her peace. After the birth, the medical staff conducted numerous tests to check that he didn't have any of the problems that Angie had, and he was absolutely fine.

Tragically, after giving birth to Theodore, Angie was given the news that her cancer treatment needed to intensify. The couple never found out whether her health had underlying problems which would have surfaced regardless of her pregnancy, or whether it was something that pregnancy had brought on. The important thing for them was that Theodore's name would remind him that he was special, that he was a gift from God and that one day he would thank God for giving him life. One day he would know that God had been looking after him despite what was going on with his mum's health, and that his name had given his parents a firm resolve during their meetings with obstetrics and haematologists.

Even as treatments proved unsuccessful, Angie kept telling her son that he was God's gift, and that he was going to be fine.

Angie was able to celebrate Theodore's first birthday with him and Christmas with the whole family in her last few weeks of life. She was thankful for every gift.

1

Knowing Me

> *Wherever the invitation of men or your own occasions lead you, speak the very truth, as your life and conscience teach it, and cheer the waiting, fainting hearts of men with new hope and new revelation.*
>
> Ralph Waldo Emerson[1]

To know your name is to know yourself.

I am frequently arrested by the way the ancient Greeks thought about things. I particularly appreciate one of their mottos engraved in stone at the Temple of Apollo at the Acropolis: 'Know thyself'. All we really want is to be known. But before others can know us, we first have to know ourselves.

This chapter will challenge you to consider the importance of your grasp of your name, the certainty of your identity.

***

We introduce ourselves with our name.

Every introduction is an invitation – an open hand extended in hope. The word 'introduction' comes from the Latin *introducere*, which means 'to lead to the inside'.[2] When you introduce yourself, you invite someone closer in. Whether and to what extent we choose to do this is up to us. As we offer ourselves as a relational gift, we portray ourselves in a way that the other might be intrigued by. How do we know if we have been successful, that the hand has been grasped, the invitation received? Through a smile, a word, or a phrase? A key indicator is whether or not our name has been remembered.

When someone remembers our name, we feel accepted; when someone forgets, we feel rejected. Our sense of identity seems so connected to our name. Your name unlocks and reveals an aspect of your identity. By fully embracing your name, looking someone straight in the eye, and then saying your name with unabashed confidence, you can instil a sense of security and peace in the individual you are meeting.

Showing interest in someone's name connects you with them on a level that may surprise both of you. In a world where we see segregation, separation, and prejudice, caring about someone's name indicates a desire to transcend race, religion and gender. This book will not tell you what to name your child, or what not to name them. Instead, it's a doorway into exploring yourself and others, so that you can gain insight into the value and significance of a name.

The opposite holds true as well: When was the last time you were in a situation where you forgot someone's name?

I panic when this happens. I want to run and hide, particularly when I have started to build some form of a relationship and I sense that the individual will be hurt. An anecdote: I had been delivering communications workshops with producers at a Fortune 100 company. Andrew (not his real name) had attended two of the training days the year before and we had really connected. I'd been asked back to deliver a day of training for twenty team members, and he was there. He greeted me warmly and as he did, he must have seen the blood drain from my face as the panic set in. With the confidence of a man who expects people to know who he is, Andrew looked me in the eye and said, 'You don't remember my name, do you?' What made this even more painful was the sadness I could detect. His eyes told me that I'd hurt him. I knew who he was, I was so pleased to see him there, but this one moment damaged the relationship. Of course, it's possible to rebuild and laugh it off, but both of us will always remember that moment.

Identity explored

Identity means 'sameness, oneness, state of being the same'[3] – it's from the Latin word *idem*: 'the same'. What is this sameness? It's a yes, an agreement. It's when someone offers you a coffee and you hadn't even realised that you actually really wanted a coffee. Drinking that coffee would meet a need that was unexpressed, unrealised, unimagined. It's not that the desire for a coffee had been suddenly put there but that an unveiling had taken place, and something that had always been there was revealed. OK, maybe that's just my love of coffee speaking, but this is identity: stepping into who you already are. And it happens in levels.

Defining your identity by what you do isn't enough, for many reasons. Many of us identify ourselves by our job. If you are a footballer and you get injured, become ill, or retire, then who are you? The key word is *are*. We should not solely define ourselves or others by what we do. Yes, the things we do mould and shape us and give us definition, but knowing who you are often requires stripping away layers of ignorance, misunderstandings, and even abuse. We have the responsibility to do this.

So, you think you know what a frisbee is? My love for frisbee was fostered playing frisbee golf in the States, nurtured on the beaches of North Wales, and kicked into serious mode with Merseyside Ultimate Club – but these activities were not why frisbees were made. Games were never intended for this wonderfully weighted, ergonomically satisfying disc. In the 1870s, William Frisbie started a baking company and the dishes he used for the pies[4] ended up being thrown around. A lot. Just because they're now used solely for throwing and have been developed into something different doesn't detract from the fact that they were originally created for something different.

Generally, it's good to know what things are made for and then relate to them as intended. My family had multiple kitchen knives bent at the tip because my dad had used them instead of a screwdriver. Some things get broken if they're not used as intended. 'Knowing me' means that we know and accept who we are. This foundation ensures our skills and contribution to society are optimised in the same way that every part of the body has a wonderful and complimentary part to play. If we live our lives outside of the sweet spot of our capabilities, we feel it.

The key to you is *not* what you do but who you are. Being used as a screwdriver doesn't make you a screwdriver.

As my friend Rudi says, 'Your identity cannot be defined. Who you are has to be experienced.' As soon as we go down this road, we're dealing with things that require faith, things that you can't necessarily define, see, or pin down, but that just are. Transcendent things, like hope.

I realised that how I lived mattered

If I asked you what your identity is, what would you say?

I was on a boat going from Penang to Langkawi in 2004 just off the coast of Malaysia, a couple of weeks before a devastating tsunami hit. As I was praying; a question formed in my mind: Why was my father proud of me? I reflected on my height, what I looked like, my sporting and academic achievements and noted that it wasn't any of those, for various reasons! I concluded that it was who I was as a human being, seen in how I related with people and how I did what I did, rather than what I did or what I looked like, that really mattered. This revelation blew me away. I recognised on a new level that I was a combination of my parents, skilfully woven together by God in a way that only He could take credit for. My parents' mandate was then to create an environment in which I could flourish and become who I had been created to be.

Do we really need to fully grasp our identity? Yes, because if we do not we can be listless, indecisive, at the mercy of the opinions of insignificant others, and are vulnerable when we go through tough times. Let me offer you hope. You are more than your successes or failures. Others may define you in relation to these – you can't stop that – but you can seek out your true identity. Your name roots you in your past and can inspire your future. It's a significant part of you that people can connect with, and it can give you a window into 'I am'.

As Thoreau wrote:

> 'I went to the woods because I wished to live deliberately, to front only the essential facts of life, and see if I could not learn what it had to teach, and not, when I came to die, discover that I had not lived. I did not wish to live what was not life – living is so dear; nor did I wish to practise resignation, unless it was quite necessary. I wanted to live deep and suck out all the marrow of life, to live so sturdily and Spartan-like as to put to rout all that was not life, to cut a broad swath and shave close, to drive life into a corner, and reduce it to its lowest terms.'[5]

My heart is that, through weighing and reflecting on ideas from this book, you will feel that you are deliberately exploring the woods of your life.

The question 'Who am I?' pushes to be addressed like a dripping tap. Failure to grapple with it affects every relationship, from family to peers, to our online interactions.

Knowing your name is foundational

'What does your name mean?' is a question I love to ask people, particularly if they have an uncommon name. Often the individual's face lights up as they recount the significance it holds, a person it represents, or a meaning that has been an anchor through the storms of life. I honestly find it thrilling when people say, 'Oh, I'm not sure… I've never really thought about it.' I may then ask them if we can have a look together – a quick search online is insightful. If they seem open to it, I may then encourage them to look for the opportunity to explore their name with their namer if possible.

A name gives insight into our namer. I was talking about this with Rudi because his parents had named him after a football player. 'Have you ever explored this with them? Why did this name resonate with them in such a way that it was given to you?' Frequently people can't answer these questions, and often the namers can't either at first.

Not really grasping your name, or having an incomplete understanding of it, can be detrimental. In the Disney film of the same name, Captain Marvel was known by the beings who discovered her after an accident as 'Vers' because her name badge had been ripped in two. It had originally read 'Danvers' and her coming to know her full name was key to her unlocking the truth of who she was. It's too shallow to define our identity in the things we do, what we own, our social status. Your identity is something to be unveiled, in the same way as gold. When pulled from the earth, it's full of impurities. The more it's put through fire, the purer and more refined it is: 9 carat; 14 carat; 18 carat; 24 carat. Likewise, we all have opportunities to become a more authentic version of ourselves as we go through times of fire in our lives. The problem is that we all hate being put through the fires of testing. As we go through them with the support of those who love us, we discover and recognise aspects of our identity, and we become more confident in saying 'I am…'.

Knowing who you are strengthens you

Gravitas is the Latin root from where we get the word gravity. It means weight, heaviness, and when I think of someone with gravitas it suggests that they have a resolute confidence in their identity.

If I was to write this:

> 'The tall man pivoted with a grace and effortlessness that belied his bulky frame. His name? James Bond.'

What would go through your mind? The theme music? A suave, sophisticated enticer of beautiful women? Or the guns, gadgets, cars and explosions due to Blovelt, his cat, and the insidious reach of Spectre? 'You know my name' was the proud boast of Chris Cornell's theme song to *Casino Royale* and yes, James Bond is a name that evokes, a name that means more than the combination of nine letters and a space. Imagine for a moment meeting him in real life. You would wonder why you were meeting him; does he want to kill you, manipulate you, or bed you?

There is something unwavering in the way it's said by Bond himself, an unapologetic confidence. He knows that by simply saying his name there will be an impact in the mind of those within earshot. Maybe it's a combination of confidence and the certainty that his reputation proceeds him. How about you? When you introduce yourself by your name is there a boldness and a certainty in it?

When you meet someone for the first time, what do you want to know? Is the priority to decide to what extent you develop a continuing relationship with them? So why do we ask what their name is – isn't this question unnecessary? In the past, a name welcomed you into a vast array of insights (we'll explore these more in chapter four) but nowadays it only provides a solitary fact, which then needs to be followed up with another question that will enable us to find out what we really want to know: 'What do you do?' However, for the majority of us, what we do doesn't, and (as I've said) shouldn't define us; what we do is simply a way of bringing in money.

Surely a better question is, 'Who are you?' If I know who you are, and I know who I am, then we can both decide how closely we want to relate to each other. Research suggests that we decide this within the first few seconds of engaging with someone. It seems that really, we're looking for ways to back up what we decided about someone before a word has left our lips. Even more critical, then, for the first thing we say to have weight, be significant, to echo a reality that is beyond what can initially be seen.

'Who am I?' is the question of the ages, and it's clear by now that I am of the opinion that exploring your name is an interesting tool to unlocking part of the answer.

Jamie Ducharme wrote an article for *Time* about why people forget names so quickly. He had interviewed Charan Ranganath, the director of the Memory and Plasticity Program at the University of California, Davis. Ranganath said, 'People are better at remembering things that they're motivated to learn'.[6] This will develop as we progress through the book, as I attempt to both stimulate and satiate your interest in names. I have found that the key to remembering names is to give a name a context, and to help build a context I use this mnemonic. In every sense, it's **APT**:

First, **ask** their name.

Then, **pause** – you may need to say, 'Can I just stop you there?'

Take a moment to **think** – of something interesting about their name. This could be someone else who has this name, a thing or colour that this name triggers in your mind, or a good follow-up question that relates to that name (this book is going to give you lots of angles for good questions).

This simple tool will have immediate benefits, both for you as well as the other. When I do this, people see that I'm interested in them and value things that matter. They also see that I'm intentional in my listening. I'm already building trust as I 'concile'. The more you do it, the quicker and easier it will become as you train your mind.

***

In order to set a foundation upon which we can explore names and naming, the following chapters will explore the power and significance of words, and then the progression from a word to a name. I'm excited about going with you on a journey, from the words that dripped like honey as they were formed by the minds of ancient thinkers to the musings of professors, NASA scientists and neighbours from my street. Why go back to ancient Greek/Roman thinking? I'll let James Turner answer that: 'The metaphorical bookworm, like its literal cousin the earthworm, loves to burrow. Imagine several bookworms patiently tunnelling down through the roots … until finally coming to the last, most deeply buried tendril. When bookworms reached bottom, they would find themselves together in the ancient Mediterranean world, listening to Greek.'[7] Throughout this book you and I are going to be those bookworms, digging deep into thoughts that have occupied thinkers for thousands of years.

2

Knowing You

But words are things, and a small drop of ink, falling like dew, upon a thought, produces that which makes thousands, perhaps millions, think.

Lord Byron[1]

To know you is only possible as you share yourself, and communication is how we share. How well do you communicate?

Words are important because they connect us to each other. They are a vehicle because they bridge the gap between me and you. Furthermore, they ensure that what is communicated can be understood and retained for others who weren't there at the time of the original communication. As human beings we are predisposed to communicate, and we use words to get to know each other. The purpose of this chapter is to explore the critical nature of words, the need to be responsible with them, and the historical background behind the origin and development of their written form. This understanding builds a foundation upon which we can more fully recognise and appreciate names.

Words capture communication and communication is the foundation of everything. To communicate means 'to give or transmit (a quality, feeling, etc.) to another' and comes from the Latin word *communicare*: 'to share, communicate, impart, inform', 'to open into each other'.[2]

Simply talking to you isn't good communication. When I communicate with you it's a two-way partnership; we offer something to each other. When you receive what I am offering, we are 'open to each other' – isn't this beautiful? So, words, and consequently names, can be the vehicle by which something that one of us *has* becomes accessible to the other.

The progress of humanity is a celebration of sharing, history being the way in which what has taken place is shared by future generations (sometimes accurately, more often than not with a certain bias). What a burden, what a weight, what a responsibility! This is one of the reasons why words are important, not only for the here and now, but also for our future. Reflecting on the importance of words will impact the way you feel about, respond to and use them.

Using words well is important

What follows is a short exchange that took place on a family walk. I was trying to use humour to stimulate one of my children into thinking about the words she was using and their impact:

> 'That Rabbit was *sick*, Dad!'
>
> Me: 'Ohhh, what a shame. I'm sure it will get better.'
>
> 'No, I mean it was cool!'
>
> Me: 'I'm sure it'll warm up; the sun's out!'

She walked off shaking her head, leaving me with a mixed sense of not knowing whether this lesson had achieved its intended outcome. On the one hand, I was pleased with myself at my outstanding wit and speed of thought, yet on the other hand, I was concerned that I had just alienated myself from my eight-year-old's world. Sowing seeds like this is giving a gift and you never know how a gift will be received.

Why would I jump on my eight-year-old's exuberant celebration of the natural world to try and make a point about words, their context, and the value of using them wisely? Because I believe passionately that words impact us far more deeply than we realise.

I reached out to Professor David Patterson in the hope of learning about the pain suffered by the Jews as their names and identity were stripped from them during the Holocaust. The Hillel Feinberg Distinguished Chair in Holocaust Studies, Professor Patterson's insights enlightened me in various ways. Here, he confirmed this sense of needing to get back to a right understanding of the value of words:

'One of the symptoms of spiritual sickness is the tearing of meaning from words. They become broken; they lose their meaning. This also has an impact on names; names lose their meaning. A word is tied to meaning. It creates a bond between one human being and another. It's an event. It's a coming together of two individuals. In a way, knowing the names of objects gives us a certain control over the object. Yes, knowing the name of the medical condition gives you a sense of control.'

Communication is the golden thread that runs through everything I do, so the precise usage and mastery of words and language are important. One of the great thinkers of history is Confucius. A note Leys writes in his translation of *The Analects of Confucius* shows the importance of words to Confucius: 'The precise use of language … sum[s] up the whole Confucian enterprise'.[3] So, what does the Confucian enterprise have to do with my daughter sharing about a rabbit and my heart for communication? As Simon Worrall says in an article for *The National Geographic*, 'Confucian thinking… [is] about a society where everyone fulfils their responsibilities and creates a harmonious situation where the whole country prospers'.[4] Confucian thinking connects ideas of harmony and countries prospering with language and words being used well. Confucius also said, 'Words are the voice of the heart'[5] – a sentiment mirrored in words from the Bible: 'the mouth speaks what the heart is full of' (Luke 6:45, NIV). What we say really is a reflection of how we feel, how we are processing the world around us and how we are able to use a set of tools to share this with those we commune with. Words link and connect, ostracise and alienate us. Could it then be said that if we grasp the importance of words, respect them, and determine ourselves to consider and use them well, that we could experience harmony with one another and see communities prosper? I believe so.

Caring about words should lead us to use them responsibly

Would you consider yourself a *philo* of *logos*? How often do you consider the words that you use, how you use them, why you use them and with whom? I would, without a second thought, say that I love (*philo*) words (*logos*) and one of my hopes for this chapter is to inspire you to love them as well. The Online Etymology Dictionary states that philology is the 'love of learning and literature; personification of linguistic and literary knowledge,'[6] and comes from the Greek word *philologia*: 'love of discussion, learning, and literature; studiousness'. Actor Stephen Campbell Moore (we'll hear more from him in chapter eight) shared his insights on this during our interview:

> 'I always find that the tension between the original meaning or root of words or names and what we actually have is a very useful thing.... For example, "decision" comes from the Latin *de caedere* which means "to cut off or kill". A lot of people don't even know what a decision is... it means slaying the other option.'[7]

The way that he highlights the importance of looking beyond the immediate is absolutely critical to the premise of this book. However, you'll have to wait until chapter eight before we really grapple with the weight of making a decision about a name. Words can be used without our really considering them, in the same way that names or the process of naming can be used or undertaken lightly.

Actually, taking a moment to consider on a deeper level what words mean has real value. It's naïve to think that the words we use will be received and interpreted the way that we intend. Words have more value than we may give them – they carry something – but also we have no control over how they are interpreted, or misinterpreted by their hearer. I believe this wholeheartedly, to the extent that there are words that are almost taboo in my house. In Proverbs we read 'One who loves discipline loves knowledge, But one who hates rebuke is stupid' (Proverbs 12:1 NASB). Even reading this 's' word in the Bible makes me feel awkward, because during workshops and sessions I have conducted, I have seen the damage it has done in people's lives. This word literally binds people up, I have had people discounting themselves and looking down on themselves even in middle age and later life because of the pain of this word.

My mum tells of a defining experience she had when she was young. After spelling 'uncle' incorrectly, she was told that she couldn't spell and was forced to stand on her chair and recite the correct spelling. Being made to feel foolish in this way is something my mum has carried throughout her life. If the teacher had been more understanding and able to teach my mum how to spell in a more accessible way, would my mum have been motivated to overcome this challenge? It was as if the teacher had placed a curse on her, the thought that bound her mind into believing that she couldn't spell became so firmly established as to be impossible to break now. We are not responsible for how the hearer of our words receives them; however, we can take responsibility for what we say. We can be reckless and uncaring about the words we use; we can ignore what they carry or the impact they can, or we can take time to examine our usage of them. A word or phrase can make us feel alive or crush us to pieces. I remember as a child the playground rhyme: 'Sticks and stones may break my bones, but words will never hurt me', and being aware while saying it that it wasn't true. How well have you developed the ability to ignore and throw off unfair or harmful words as well as embrace accurate and edifying ones?

Words can add colour to written or spoken communication and particularly inspiring ones can be sourced from a thesaurus. *Thesaurus* is actually a Latin word itself; it means 'storehouse of treasures'! 'The beautiful locks of your radiant hair thrill me as they dance across your neck with complexity and fluidity' sounds much more engaging than 'your hair looks nice'. There's something compelling about exploring and utilising words, so fall in love with them again, and maybe go treasure hunting!

Written text and the development of humanity

If words can have such an impact, then surely recording them is a gift and a danger, both for the one who forms them as well as the one who receives them.

Humanity has always desired to communicate effectively; the origin and development of written words has been a key component in every step in our advancement. Let's see how foundational thinkers from global civilisations have tracked this.

Communication started as soon as there were two. One would have wanted to share with the other; one human had to indicate to another human that they wanted to share something. Let's imagine our primitive ancestors pointing at something, like a deer, then at their mouth, maybe to indicate 'I want to eat that – let's kill it'. We have to start with what we have: early paintings and engravings. Found all over the world, it was the San or 'Bushmen' who left them in various parts of my beloved South Africa. Rock art is found near Citrusdal, an amazing town in the heart of the Cederberg Wilderness. I visited there one June, which is the peak season for fruit. As the name suggests, Citrusdal isn't primarily known for its wine, fishing, or hot water springs (which are also a wonderful reason to visit), but for the plethora of globally acclaimed oranges, grapefruit, and naartjies that flourish there. I was able to see first-hand some of the most wonderfully painted images – hunters and their prey, elephants and bok tramping and leaping across the receptive red rock – while quenching my thirst with juice from freshly squeezed local produce. These images could have been an expression of respect, love, admiration, celebration, or maybe the artist's favourite food. History is voiceless to inform us; however, we can infer that the artist is sharing, communicating. After all, they were speaking to me in that cave, and now to you as you read this chapter.

So, what was the first step of written communication? To find out the origin of an alphabet, we have to start with Egyptian hieroglyphics dating back to around 3000 BC.

In his book *The Alphabet Versus the Goddess*,[8] Leonard Shlain shows us that the images (glyphs) used by the Egyptians had three functions:

'(1) to represent the image of a thing or action, (2) to stand for the sound of a syllable, and (3) to clarify the precise meaning of adjoining glyphs'. Egyptian tradition says that their god Thoth gave hieroglyphics to the Egyptians to 'make them wiser and to strengthen their memory'.

In the early 19th century, Jean-François Champollion and James Turner unravelled the mystery of hieroglyphics by using the Rosetta Stone and an obelisk from Philae. Professor JC Darnell of Yale University drew back the veil to show me how hieroglyphics progressed into the first alphabet in the early Bronze Age (1850 – 1700 BC) with scratches of shapes on rock discovered at the Wadi el-Hôl in Egypt:

> 'The Wadi el-Hôl texts, then, would be among the earliest (if not the earliest) specimen of alphabetic writing discovered to date.... The Wadi el-Hôl inscriptions, as two of the earliest alphabetic inscriptions, thus provide the crucial link that conclusively proves the derivation of early alphabetic signs from both hieratic and hieroglyphic Egyptian writing. ... Of course, any speculation about the precise context in which alphabetic writing first emerged should not be pressed too hard, given the paucity of early alphabetic texts and the still highly impoverished state of these texts' decipherment.'[9]

Exploring Professor Darnell's work was like stepping into an Indiana Jones film – a university professor who discovered ancient things from a time almost forgotten that give insight into the foundations of our written world.

Enmerkar and the Lord of Aratta was written in Mesopotamia, (seen as a cradle of learning and wisdom) around 1800 BC. It gives us the first known story of writing a text:

> 'His speech was substantial, and its contents extensive. The messenger, whose mouth was heavy, was not able to repeat it. Because the messenger, whose mouth

was tired, was not able to repeat it, the lord of Kulaba patted some clay and wrote the message as if on a tablet. Formerly, the writing of messages on clay was not established. Now, under that sun and on that day, it was indeed so.'[10]

There it is, a communication captured on clay, available for whoever wanted to read it, ponder over it, refer to it from that point on, knowing another took a massive step forward.

Who was the lord of Kulaba? Well, he must have been the individual in charge of Kulaba, which is also known as Ulug Kulaba, Uruk, and was quite possibly Erech, a city founded by Nimrod, a character found in the Jewish Torah, Bereishith (Genesis) Chapter 10.[11] It's believed that this city was 30 km east of the city of Samawah in modern Iraq.

As we continue to trace the history of capturing words as a way to deepen knowing, we come to the Greeks, in the fifth century BC. The harnessing of the power of words completely exploded through the Greek and Roman civilisations leading to massive strides in knowing each other, communication and education in general. In *Cratylus*, Plato is teaching about how words and names are the tools we use to express the nature of things to one another. We are going to explore the name part fully in a later chapter, but for the time being, note that Plato emphasises their importance:

> 'All names … are intended to show the nature of things … let me ask another question: If we had no faculty of speech, how should we communicate with one another? Should we not use signs, like the deaf and dumb? …What, then, is a name? In the first place, a name is not a musical, or, secondly, a pictorial imitation, but an imitation of that kind which expresses the nature of a thing; and is the invention not of a musician, or of a painter, but of a namer.'[12]

By stripping words down to their component parts, we can grasp what they are before we then put them together and use them. Did you notice the way that Plato compares the act of communication that is shared between a musician, a painter, a writer and a namer? I will at points throughout this book look at these forms of communication and also compare them, using them to bring to light the depth and varying levels of communication that they hold for those of us who earnestly seek to 'live deep and suck out all the marrow of life' as Thoreau said; to really grapple with and engage with that which is being shared with us.

Words have always mattered

It's easy to see why Plato is so highly regarded; his use of words to distil complex thoughts was revolutionary. However, how would a lay person realise some of the golden threads Plato weaves through his work? How can we increase in our knowing as we grapple with his words? Ironically for most of us, the words he communicates with and a personal exploration of *Cratylus* would be beyond our capacity, which is why reflections from the Project Gutenberg e-book on *Cratylus* are so helpful.

> 'Words appear to be isolated, but they are really the parts of an organism which is always being reproduced. They are refined by civilization, harmonized by poetry, emphasized by literature, technically applied in philosophy and art; they are used as symbols on the border-ground of human knowledge; they receive a fresh impress from individual genius, and come with a new force and association to every lively-minded person. They are fixed by the simultaneous utterance of millions, and yet are always imperceptibly changing; – not the inventors of language, but writing and speaking, and particularly great writers, or works which pass into the hearts of nations, Homer, Shakespeare, Dante, the German or English Bible,

Kant and Hegel, are the makers of them in later ages. They carry with them the faded recollection of their own past history; the use of a word in a striking and familiar passage gives a complexion to its use everywhere else, and the new use of an old and familiar phrase has also a peculiar power over us.'[12]

Even this quote is like chewing on a piece of steak… allow me to further pre-digest for you; words are being portrayed here as living things, they adapt change and are refined by those that use them. They seem fixed but are constantly changing and have a power to carry an idea or change ideas over a period of time. I find this exploration of words compelling, along with the idea of their foundational and timeless value.

***

My final thought is also one of the most important to me personally, and, despite many attempts remains unchangeably significant. The Bible, arguably the foundational text of Western civilization, personifies words. Words may in fact change in their meaning, so to know a word, you have to experience a relationship with it, which takes us back to what Rudi says – to know me, you have to experience me. 'In the beginning was the Word, and the Word was with God, and the Word was God' (John 1:1 NASB).

As we reflect on where words came from and how ancient cultures began to string them together, we begin to understand how foundational they are to our present-day communication.

Please take time to consider these questions: Are you grateful for words? Are you glad that you have the tools to express something that is in your heart that has the ability to inspire, create and give hope? Have you experienced being hurt or healed by them and why?

Do you find it compelling that a love for words demands us to respect them and to at times be wary of them? Does harbouring an awareness of the impact they make lead to a sense of reverence for them or vulnerability towards them in you? What motivates or restricts your communication? How could this be a reflection on how you feel about yourself and sharing yourself with others?

I hope that this chapter has stimulated your thinking regarding words and communication. If so, I believe this will have ensured that, as we start to think about the difference between a word and a name, you will elevate your relationship with names. This is what words do, they elevate, they widen and broaden, and your name is a word. It's a word that somehow captures the essence of the giver of the name and subsequently carries a significant facet of your identity.

3

Knowing Things

I confused things with their names: that is belief.
Jean-Paul Sartre[1]

We name things because we know them. Well, that's how it's intended to be.

The Judeo-Christian tradition teaches that God gave humanity the mandate to name. Humans were distinct within all creation in their ability to discern the very nature of a created thing due to their ability to relate with it and its maker.

> 'And out of the ground the Lord God formed every animal of the field and every bird of the sky, and brought *them* to the man to see what he would call them; and whatever the man called a living creature, that was its name' (Genesis 2:19 NASB).

What was the last thing you felt moved to name?

I watched Disney's *Monsters Inc* last night. The two principal characters (Sully and Mike, both monsters) were discussing a human that one of them (Sully) had developed a fondness for. The child's name was Mary, but Sully (unaware of her name) called her 'Boo'. The other monster, Mike, was a lot more practical and was horrified that Sully had connected with a human, and worse, that he had given it a name! He told Sully that he shouldn't have named 'it', because once you give something a name you start to become attached to it. Mike was right; but also wrong. Sully had named Boo because he had already become attached to her; he cared about her.

When we name things it's because we have become more attached to them; they have become more significant to us. Without being given a name by them, Boo would have existed, but she would have held less significance in their world, the relationship would have been different.

In this chapter we are going to consider how a name is a word that becomes the tool to explore and define our relationship with that which is 'other'. When we talk about a thing by name, we commune with it. As human beings we have a compulsion to name things because we recognise that they are separate from us, they are 'other'. We can choose to ignore them, but our bodies have clearly been designed to engage with and relate to that which is other.

We have explored how significant words can be. They have the ability to give life to someone and to tear down just as easily. The example with my mother and her teacher was simple, but reports of suicide due to bullying are tragic and not uncommon, as are instances where a kind word or a thoughtful encouragement have brought healing. If words can have this impact, what about names?

Have you ever felt drawn to something? Ever had some sense of connection with something that warranted a deepening of the relationship? For example, it's easy to move from 'car' to 'Fiat 500'. Then there's the moment when the car starts to feel like it means something to you; it's your first car, or you go on holiday in it, its braking system ensures you avoid an accident, or it's the location of a first kiss. The reward? You decide to name it 'Sky' because it's light blue, or 'Wayne' because of your reading of the number plate WA18YNE. We name all sorts of things, from cats and dogs to buildings – even body parts.

In the introduction to their book *Names and Naming*, Puzey and Kostanski say that names 'influence our perceptions of ourselves and others, of places near and far; they inform or reinforce social practices; and, contrary to the inferences of Shakespeare's Juliet ("A rose by any other name would smell as sweet"), names can play a role in defining the quality of the objects they denote'.[2] I like the idea that names in some way define the quality of an object, that they carry something that is understood, to a greater or lesser extent, by the hearer as well as the speaker. So, does this elevate them above simple words?

'Words have meaning and names have power' is a quote attributed to 17th century Spanish author Miguel de Cervantes Saavedra, who penned the novel *Don Quixote*. It suggests a difference between words and names (nouns). Let's separate a noun from a proper noun.

'The thing is hungry' – the noun (thing) creates no connection for us with the subject, it feels distant and dismissive.

'The dog is hungry' – the noun (dog) connects us to the subject. We can relate to it through our experience of dogs; this can be positive or negative.

'Buster, the dog, is hungry' – we have a proper noun (Buster), which suddenly invites us into a relationship. The dog has a name, which seems to make it more relatable. We reason that it has a namer and so it has at some point experienced connection with a human.

Which of these three would you feed: a thing, a dog, or a dog called Buster? Why?

Let's explore some of the roles names play, how they are connected to relationships, our ability to relate and the use and abuse of power.

We name things as a tool to remember

An aspect to naming, mentioned in the previous chapter, was illustrated in the mandate of Thoth the Egyptian god of hieroglyphics: 'To make us wiser and aid our memory'.

I love the true sense of the word 'remember'. It breaks down into 're' and 'member', so I see remembering as putting things together again, in the same way a surgeon would stitch parts of the body that had been separated back together so that the body can be whole again.

This is no better seen than in the naming of buildings and streets. Walking down local streets is somewhat of a history lesson for those of a curious disposition. My favourite is the audacity of the Welsh builders Owen Elias and his son, William Owen Elias, who were building houses here in Liverpool in the 19th century. They used the first initials of their names for 22 streets along Goodison Road and County Road:

Oxton, Winslow, Eton, Neston, Andrew, Nimrod, Dane, Wilburn,

Ismay, Lind, Lowell, Index, Arnot, Makin, Olney, Weldon, Euston, Nixon, Elton, Liston, Imrie, and Astor.

I wondered what the guidelines were now compared to when these streets were named, so I asked George Kwok, Assistant Engineer in Highways and Transportation at Liverpool City Council. He told me this:

> 'In our 'Street Naming Guidance' we try to get developers to put forward names that are linked either historically to the site or community. The intention is to have names of more interest/relevance/etcetera to each particular location but, unfortunately, more often than not, developers are unable to put forward names with such links. Of course, not allowing duplication or partial duplication of existing street names (plus the other criteria such as no names of people) also limits what new street names can be progressed.'

The goal is clearly to have names that locals can relate to because even street names matter; it's an initiative that helps to develop a sense of local identity through understanding relationships. Much has been done in Liverpool as residents reflect on the names of streets that 'aid our memory' of people who were involved in the shipping slave trade. An effective but horrific triangle, this route went from major European ports to West Africa and then on to America before returning to complete the trip. Liverpool's connection to the slave trade as a key dock runs deep, and this blood-soaked heritage is observed in some of the names of the streets. The then Lord Mayor of Liverpool, Cllr Anna Rothery, explained the responsibility of weighing legacy names during our interview:

> 'The issue of streets around Liverpool that have been named after former slave masters is a huge topic. We have been asking how the naming of a street that's associated with a horrendous history in terms of

enslavement impact individuals today who are living in and walking those streets and see these names as a constant reminder of a history that is still painful for many of us.'[3]

Cllr Rothery's thoughts illustrate the weight of responsibility undertaken when naming and how, in this instance, there are regularly updated guidelines in place to advise and hopefully protect against future pain because the name of a street matters. This sense of responsibility is further explored in chapter eight when we reflect on the weight of naming a human.

A name gives something value

Many years ago, we had a beautiful dog named Shani and wanted to give her the chance to have puppies. As this was to be a significant experience for all of us, we decided that it should be a positive one, undertaken with a wise and experienced pair of hands. As I looked into the arrangement of an appropriate liaison, I entered into an extraordinary world. I won't go into the ins and outs of the experience, but it wasn't candles and Barry White. The male was of particularly good stock, and when going over his paperwork as well as the paperwork for the puppies, I was taken by the significance of the names. Shani's pedigree name was 'Dashing with Dasher', which I didn't understand. Her name was her pedigree; it was a name that opened a door into five generations of dogs, all Shani's various relations. 'Dashing with Dasher' connected her with her heritage in a similar way to which our names often connect us with ours. Her name connected her with her context and the context provided value because it gave her credibility. She wasn't just a dog, she was daughter of, related to, descended from, and loved by. Her true value was in our relationship with her, but her pedigree name mattered, as it gave her value in both a historical and a financial sense.

A name elevates an object

There are many things in my home, but I don't give them individual names. At this moment, my eyes fall on my salt and pepper grinders. My grinders don't have names. Why? Don't they deserve a name? I wonder if Jamie Oliver has ever named a cooking utensil… If I was a chef and had a frying pan that had been handed down from generations of chefs, maybe it would have a name.

I have always been taken by the naming of swords in *The Lord of the Rings*. Bilbo and Frodo were saved on more than one occasion due to the sword Sting. Gandalf wielded the sword Glamdring, which means 'Foe-hammer' and Andúril was the re-forged sword for Aragorn. Its name meant 'Flame of the West' which spoke of how Aragorn (from the West) would deal with his enemies. Paul Mortimer, one of the editors of the book *The Sword in Anglo-Saxon England from the 5th to 7th century*, explains:

> 'Swords are very special. They're not like any other weapons; they're specifically for killing human beings. Swords have no other practical purpose, although their display will tell the observer much about the status of the wearer. … In Old English literature there are only three swords that are definitely named. Two in Beowulf and one in a fragment of another poem, Waldere. It may be that many men named their swords but that the name was between the man and his weapon; he told no one else. There are lots of quite renowned weapons that we aren't told the names of, and it may be that like the modern car, some people like to name their cars, but most probably don't.'[4]

It's unfortunate that the names of swords were not recorded more frequently. If they had been, we would have more insight into the men who wielded the weapons.

We delve further into naming swords in chapter nine where we consider another swordsmith's experiences while crafting swords, but the key is that an item that is named is clearly valued above other unnamed things. I have found no records of anyone naming a scabbard, a toothbrush, or a handkerchief. Perhaps they don't matter as much.

A name elicits a sense of ownership

Naming can imply ownership, but there's a key difference between giving your name to something and giving it its own name. In the Disney film *Toy Story*, one of the characters takes great comfort in knowing that he has the name of the boy that he belongs to written on his boot; it made the toy feel like it mattered to the child. The child had written his name on the foot of the toy but didn't call the toy by that name. How about other, more significant things where ownership can be disputed? Why did early explorers like Columbus or John Cabot feel that they had the right to name the places they 'discovered', and by so doing exert some kind of claim on them? Indigenous Māori already knew New Zealand as Aotearoa, so in what way did Tasman have the right to rename it? There is a global awareness of and movement towards the renaming of places in light of their original cultural heritage – a realisation that others had no right to impose a name on something when those who had a relationship with it had already named it out of that relationship. This can also be a form of abuse, seen in slave owners giving their slaves their name – a source of pain I have spoken about with people from the West Indies. Giving a name to something you have no right to is an abuse of power, because naming matters, it's powerful.

How about stars? I remember looking at options for a unique Christmas presents years ago and discovering that you could name a star. I was thrilled at the thought that somehow you could have something as significant as a star named after you. I imagined looking up into the night sky and thinking, 'That's my star out there'. There's a sense of power to that, and in order to do that I would pay money, if I had enough money that would give me the power to do that, or maybe if I had a certain political office or a certain number of 'followers'. But can one really name a star? On what grounds would someone believe that they have the right to sell such a claim in the first place? I wondered who did have that power, the authority to name stars. Researching this question led me to the International Astronomical Union (IAU) and ultimately to a conversation with the chair of the committee that actually names stars. Professor Mamajek, Chair and organiser of the IAU Division C Working Group on Star Names explained the extraordinary lengths they go to to ensure that they don't misuse power, but look to honour global cultures and traditions that had already developed relationships with them:

> 'We realised that we were at this point in history where we're finding these new planets around the stars. If we're going to start naming these, then some of the orbit stars already have names and we have to explore and vet the historical and cultural astronomy in literature to standardise those because you don't want to write over these names. You don't want to take your ship to Greenland and then call it Prince William Island, or something like that – it's already got a name. You don't want to rename something that's already been named.'

I shared with him about my thoughts on how naming actually develops a relationship with a thing, and he agreed:

> 'Yes, at first it's a thing you're interacting with. There's a gradation in the reality of how much you can grasp about an individual object… When it becomes a series of dots, and whether those are asteroids, comets or dwarf planets moving in the sky, it becomes special. They will stitch together those observations and look for matches with others. After several steps it gets a number, then it's eligible for naming. We can point to

it, we can send a spacecraft to it, it has longstanding value. You see this with celestial objects, you get to know them better and better, and they go from just being a pinprick of light to a place that we become familiar with. Ceres is covered with craters and hills and valleys and now there's a whole set of nomenclature on it. And now we get to study it scientifically and we can tell a story, where it fits within the history of the solar system, and now within the scientific community we talk about Ceres and people know what we're talking about.'

There seems to be a delicate balance between naming in terms of relationship and ownership. The more the relationship developed, the more the entity mattered, which in a sense proved that it deserved to have a name. It had become important to those who were relating with it, as we see in this next section.

A name recognises the importance of something

If something has no name, can it even be considered to have importance? This was one of the drivers behind the work of Professor Quentin Wheeler and something that he hopes will inspire future entomologists (people who study insects). He shared this with me:

'The first beetle I named was Isoplastus uncus, a tiny round beetle that I collected on a trip to Mexico when I was an undergraduate student. Naming my first organism was a moment I'll never forget. For me, the real intellectual thrill is that moment of recognition when you realise, wow, this is a new species... then it becomes kind of real when you assign a name to it. Which is important, because how serious can we be about wanting to save other species if we don't care enough about them to give them a name? Is anyone really going to care if they're just a statistic? If you know that there are a thousand species in this particular family, why should you care if that number is 1000 or 999, but once you give it a name and sort of put a face on it, I think it changes the game entirely. I think we're making a huge mistake by not accelerating the process of naming species at this particular moment in time when they're facing a mass extinction. We've only named maybe 20% of the world's animals and plants! Even the ones that are going to go extinct, we know that we're not going to save them all, we know we're going to lose some, but I think that we still owe it to honour them enough to give them a name before they go.'

We'll hear more from Professor Wheeler later in the book as he shares the difference he experienced between naming a species of insect and naming his children. We name things to show their importance, that they aren't worthless and transient, but that they matter.

I've always found it strange that storms and significant weather events are given names. In his book *Brain Droppings*, comedian George Carlin writes (apologies if you find the humour dark):

'Do you know why hurricanes have names instead of numbers? To keep the killing personal. No one cares about a bunch of people killed by a number. "200 Dead as Number Three Slams Ashore" is not nearly as interesting a headline as "Charlie kills 200". Death is much more satisfying and entertaining if you personalize it. Me, I'm still waitin' for Hurricane Ed. Old Ed wouldn't hurt ya, would he? Sounds kinda friendly. "No, we ain't evacuatin'. Ed's comin'!"'[5]

Naming storms is actually important. During the storm season of 1953, the United States started to use female names for storms, and by the late 1970s, both male and female names were being used. The key was identification: short, easily remembered names used through written and spoken communication mediums was quicker and reduced confusion when storms were occurring frequently. The World Meteorological Organization further clarified and established naming procedures, so Atlantic hurricanes have a list of potential male and female names which are used on a six-year rotation.[6] If, however, a storm is extremely violent and its effects are significantly tragic in terms of lives or structural devastation, the use of its name for a subsequent storm could be considered inappropriate. On these grounds a country can petition the World Meteorological Organization to retire a name. This tragically reveals what a catastrophic year 2017 was; records show that four names were retired: Nate – Central America, United States Gulf Coast; Maria – Lesser Antilles, Puerto Rico; Irma – Caribbean, Southeastern United States; and Harvey – Texas, Louisiana. So here we see that a name gives us an ability to identify with a thing, to in recognition of an attribute in its character or personality.

Giving a name indicates a relationship

Very few of us would consider the implications of naming a mountain, never mind having to summit it in the first place. Explorer Bryan Jackson told me:

> 'I have had the great privilege of climbing previously unclimbed mountains in three separate continents. A lot of unclimbed mountains are named by the governments of their respective countries, so you do not have the opportunity to name them even though you are the first to climb them. To trek where no one has ever trekked before is amazing; to summit a mountain no one has climbed before is phenomenal; but then to be allowed to name the mountain forever is mindblowing and a real responsibility. It will be named in perpetuity, and it is a legacy of sorts. There

is a sense of gravity in naming a permanent feature on the landscape, a permanence. This name will be used by future mountaineers, by the map services and recorded in the Himalayan Database. It is a privilege but also needs some thought and cannot just be trivial. It will only ever be adopted in use by the locals if there was previously no name and they are happy with the name. In Nepal for example the locals have lived close to the mountains for hundreds of years, so it is important to bear that in mind when naming a mountain, to follow any local traditions and to be sensitive to the region.'

Throughout our conversation I heard about how names that he gave had been adopted by the locals. I believe that this was because of the relationship that he had developed with them as much as the actual name he had bestowed. There were no records or tribal histories of anyone else ever feeling the need to name these unclimbed, uninhabited features. Their naming and the tribal acceptance of the name (demonstrated in subsequent visits) illustrated the relationship between the locals and the mountain, that it had a name by which they related with it.

A name can declare the nature of something

An article from *The Guardian* newspaper centred around a New Zealand entomologist[7] who had named a wasp after a character from the Harry Potter books by JK Rowling, so of course I reached out to him. Dr Saunders told me that he was interested in taxonomy – the discovery, classification, naming, and relationships between distinct species. He wanted to show that not all of New Zealand's 3000+ species of wasps were bad, so had started by naming a parasitoid wasp *Lusius malfoyi*:

'Most names are descriptive; they will tell you something of the biology, the anatomy or behaviour. The dominant narrative is that wasps are bad; they sting people, and they are awful. I wanted to do something a little different and try to change people's perception a little bit about wasps, entomology and taxonomy. The fictional namesake (Lucius) and his family (Malfoy) have a sinister reputation in the Harry Potter stories. However, in the end their reputations are salvaged. The point was that we want people to look at wasps in a different way, as well as to help people realise that it's only a small percentage that sting or do damage.'

I was so impressed by how Dr Saunders had used a name to guide us into a better relationship with this organism through a better understanding of its nature. Here was a concrete, scientific example of the impact of naming something purposefully.

***

In each of these instances we have seen how a name alters our relationship with something and that being a namer carries responsibility and has ramifications. But how does this compare with naming a child? When we name a child, are we declaring our ownership of it? Are we showing its value or classifying it in some way? Are we showing that it has a level of importance or significance that it would not otherwise have, or is naming a child completely different? Could it be that Dr Saunders was tapping into a next level of naming where the name isn't simply a description to categorise, but the expression of an insight into, or a statement about, the essence of the nature of something? Bear in mind that Saunders named a species, not every individual wasp within that species. Giving a name to an individual organism could only be the role of a namer who has that position or level of relationship. This is what we will explore next.

How about you? How has this chapter encouraged you to wonder at the names you give things, or caused you to reflect on why you named your first car? There is a safety in bestowing a name on something that can only receive it. That's what makes naming things comparatively easy. In later chapters we will explore what happens when someone acts on their freedom to reject the name they've been given.

Words are significant in that they are the vehicle that we use to connect with that which is other, that which surrounds us. We live our lives with varying levels of intentionality, and when we recognise the value of words and their role in establishing and clarifying the way we interact with our world, everything is elevated.

As we move into the second part of this book, we are going to build on this foundation as we examine the process of naming human beings, explore why it differs from naming other things, and rediscover the universal acceptance of the importance of naming.

Introduction to Part Two

If you were to look at the Mona Lisa, a quite simple engagement with it would be to say whether you liked it or not, what you thought about the colours, her clothes and her smile (or whatever her expression is). The next level would be to explore how the painting made you feel, or maybe search on Google to see what others say about it. The painting may make you feel peaceful or curious; you might reflect on what she could be feeling or wonder what it would be like to be captured and known based on one look, and subsequently judged throughout history. A third level of engagement would come from discovering what was in the heart of the painter when it was painted. What was Leonardo Da Vinci feeling when he painted it? Was it painted in a time of joy, loss, despair, hope? How is the essence of the artist communicated in the brush strokes? Was he wanting to share something with us through the painting?

How is the essence of a namer communicated in the naming? Is the name given more valuable if the namer has considered it at length? Is the painting more valuable if it has been painted by a renowned painter or by someone who is simply trying to express something they're feeling?

All three of my children painted in their younger years. Did these pieces come from a place of understanding what they were 'going through' at the time, or were they just painting? Does a painter who has grieved her way through a painting make the work more valuable through this process than the painting my daughter did? I don't think so. However, communion happens when a painting is shared. When my child shows me her painting, she shares her experience or something she is processing. 'Look daddy, a butterfly!' She has connected with the butterfly, and she then wants to share that connection with me. She does this through the medium of painting. She could also write a poem, compose a song, or maybe choreograph a dance. Why does she want to do this, though? Because she knows that something happens between us when she does. The knitting of hearts is important to her. Is my communion with her of less value than the communion I experience with, for example, my dad, because it's childlike and innocent, less thought-out and considered? No, but there would be a deeper, different level with my dad if we were discussing a painting that he had created. It would be richer, more complex, like a fine wine that has been well aged. So, who do you want to commune with? Do you go to the painting to commune with the artist? When we commune and share, what is the benefit for us? What if the artist doesn't want to commune?

How then does this correlate with giving a name? Does a more considered name have more value than a name that somehow 'just came' to the namer, or one which was simply the name of the midwife? I don't think it means *more*; the important realisation is that there has been a connection. We explore this more in the second part of the book.

Reflect again on this quote from Plato that I referred to in chapter two – 'What, then, is a name? A name is not a musical or a pictorial communing, but one which expresses the heart. And it's not the expression of a musician, or of a painter, but of a namer.'

4

To Research a Name

I hate ridiculous names; my weird name has haunted me all my life.

Peaches Geldof[1]

How much research has gone into your name?

How much consideration should go into the process of researching a name, and at what point would one be judged as qualified to be a namer? The introduction to this part suggested that all that mattered was the heart, that my daughter's painting has as much value to me as a famous artist's. In this sense then, so should a name, it's the most significant gift given to a child, and comes from a heart of love. A name chosen after significant investment of time should be valued with the same regard as one that seems to just appear at the right moment, at the moment of naming. After exploring these next chapters, perhaps you will have become more resolute in your opinion, or perhaps it will have changed.

The previous chapter encouraged you to look at how objects or other things have names and why that may be. In this chapter we're finishing the foundation on which the heart of the book can be built. We need to look at human names. We will explore what names mean, why they mean certain things to certain people, and discover if they can help or hinder us through life. We will examine whether picking the 'right' or 'wrong' name guarantees success or condemns us to failure, relationally or financially. This chapter will be divided into two sections. The first section researches where names have come from and how they have developed. The second section is about how a name affects those who hear it.

***

One of the most famous meditations on names, was written by William Shakespeare in the tragedy *Romeo and Juliet*[2]:

> O Romeo, Romeo, wherefore art thou Romeo?
> Deny thy father and refuse thy name,
> Or if thou wilt not, be but sworn my love,
> And I'll no longer be a Capulet.
> 'Tis but thy name that is my enemy,
> Thou art thyself, though not a Montague.
> What's Montague? It is not hand, nor foot,
> Nor arm, nor face, nor any other part
> Belonging to a man. O, be some other name.
> What's in a name? That which we call a rose
> By any other word would smell as sweet,
> So Romeo would, were he Romeo not called.
> Retain that dear perfection which he owes
> Without that title. Romeo, doff thy name,
> And for thy name, which is no part of thee,
> Take all myself.

There's a yearning in Juliet. She will give her very self if he would simply drop his name ("'Tis but thy name that is my enemy'). After all, 'What's in a name? That which we call a rose by any other word would smell as sweet.' Beautifully innocent Juliet is trying to assure Romeo that there is a separation between his name and his identity, just as there would be between a rose and its name. Romeo responds by echoing the object of his affection's blind desire and replies, 'Call me but love, and I'll be new baptised.' However, the tragedy is that they do not escape the shadowy noose of their names, as their names are about more than a word. They convey family, belonging, responsibilities, and are steeped in history, tensions and rivalry, forces that shape their destiny beyond a mere label.

How about you? Have you ever considered whether you would smell as sweet by another name? Would you be more attractive to a prospective partner if you were called Juan or Claudia? Would you have gotten that promotion at work if your name sounded more white-collar, like Elizabeth or Sebastian?

Philip means 'lover of horses'. Does this mean that every person named Philip is automatically predisposed to love horses? What if you're called Philip and you hate horses? Were you given the wrong name? Maybe you were traumatised by a horse when you were younger or experienced the pain of *Black Beauty* far too deeply? One of my interviewees put it like this:

> 'I remember meeting a nurse called Mercy, and she had none! So, what does William mean? And the reason I have to ask that is that it's not immediately obvious. If you are called Constance or Ernest, they're very obvious descriptions. I'm not saying that you expect someone called Constance to be constant, or you expect someone called Earnest to be particularly earnest, but it's fascinating. I feel like our journey is to find out our own identity to some degree, both as a part of the world that we live in and also within ourselves; they are both parts of the same thing. Part of a lot of people's journeys is coming to terms with the name that they've been prescribed.'

Here are some of the questions I want to explore in this chapter: Everyone decries prejudice; however, what if by simply giving a child a certain name you could ensure that they thrived? Isn't one generation's greatest desire to ensure the provision and protection of successive generations? Can a name bring covering in the way that laws and societies' sense of obligation can never do? Can the gender inference of your name affect your job prospects? How fashionable is your name and why do names drop in and out of fashion? What would you discover if you were to look up your first name and surname and explore its history, and would discovering that you were descended from Polynesian farmers or Celtic warriors change you? I remember how thrilled my 6'4" tree-felling, cottage-building, family-loving, lamb-on-a-spit-consuming hulk of a friend Murray was when he discovered that his surname was of Norman origin and how he, fittingly, was probably descended from Vikings.

Given names

Where did names come from? Let's imagine that we were transported back in time to a small, rural community somewhere in the green windswept fields of what is now known as Croydon, south of London; back to a time when in order to distinguish between members of the community, we named them. What would we name them? Where an individual was the tallest, we could refer to him as 'Tall', in which case I would say, 'I was talking to Tall', and you would know who I meant. Or we could relate to someone by what she did; let's say she was the baker: 'I was talking to Baker'. This makes sense. However, at what point was 'Tall' tall? What was he called as a baby?! Did 'Baker' start folding pastry and crumbling a mix of flour and butter over rhubarb following her emergence from her mother's womb?

In most of our European cultures as well as cultures that have been significantly affected by European thinking, the given name, also known as a 'Christian name', 'forename' or 'first name' usually comes before the family name. Traditionally, however, the family name comes first in Hungary, parts of Africa and most of East Asia, for example China and Japan. We are going to explore European thinking in this chapter and hear about global naming traditions and practices in a subsequent chapter.

Given names have originally come from all manner of things:

Locations – Paris, Devon.

Jobs – George apparently means 'farmer'. However contrary to popular thought, Doug has nothing to do with developing trenches. We had a florist called Rosie preparing the flowers for our wedding, which made me wonder how many florists have floral names?

Nature – Oak, Ivy, Briar, Rose, Poppy, Skye.

Times and dates – April, Wednesday, Natalie ('born on Christmas

Day'). The Ghanaian Nobel Peace Prize-winning Secretary General of the United Nations, Kofi Annan, was a wonderful human being whose name means 'born on Friday'.

Combinations – in some South African cultures there is a tradition to give children a name that is a combination of the parent's names. I remember teaching a girl called Lemarsh, whose mother was Lesley and father was Marshal. My friend Geordon Rendle was named after his mum Georgia and his dad Donald, in what Geordon describes as an 'intentionally creative reflection of their love!'

Faith or religious references have significant connotations, although they can be controversial: Mary was considered too holy to be used by the public until the twelfth century and Mohammed and Jesus are also treated with honour. Being given the name Jesus is common in Spanish circles yet could be seen as blasphemous in others. Muslim names can be Abd-Allah (servant of God), or Aadil, which means just, or upright. Hebrew names are very common due to the biblical root of Christian nations and include Adam, Eve, Caleb, Joshua, Benjamin, Reuben and Tamar.

There are international names that have retained popularity such as Henry, Charles, Robert, Edward and Alfred.

Mononyms

A monoym is a singular name. Benedict Cumberbatch encounters one in a film where he deliciously replies to Wong the librarian while portraying Marvel's enigmatic Dr Strange. He looks to clarify if Wong has any other names, or whether he is simply known by this monoym, like Adele or Bono.

Monoyms are observable throughout history, although often we are gifted with epithets for clarity, for example Zeno of Elea and Zeno the Stoic. I think Zeno is a brilliant name. Since both were Greek philosophers, how have they been distinguished from each other? The former was born around 490 BC and would have been found chewing the philosophical fat with Plato, Parmenides and Socrates. He is acknowledged for his paradoxes and is labelled 'of Elea', a Greek founded coastal town in the Salerno region of Italy, now known as Velia. The latter, Zeno the Stoic, came 100 years later and his stoicism promoted an emphasis on goodness and peace of mind, drawn from living an apparently virtuous life in harmony with nature. It's interesting that one is described by his geographical origin, the other by his philosophy.

Some monyms are chosen by their owners. I remember my confusion as a nine-year-old while feverishly opening packs of Mexico 86 stickers for my World Cup sticker album. Whenever I unpacked a Brazilian football player, they had no surnames, players like Pele and Zico. History suggests that the extraordinary 18th century French writer Voltaire never explained the reasoning behind his nom de plume (pen name). However, there are all manner of theories to do with what the word might mean, or to what extent the dropping of his name was a rejection of his father's values. Ira Wade really invested into this by writing a 19-page journal article on the subject, exploring twelve different theories banded about in the 18th and 19th centuries.[3] The confused intrigue harboured by many a bibliophile was tellingly expressed in the apparent altercation between Guy-August de Rohan and Voltaire on meeting at the opera towards the end of January 1726: 'Mons de Voltaire, Mons Arouet, comment vous appelez-vous?'[4] which means: 'Mr Voltaire, Mr Arouet, what is your name?' Or perhaps, more tellingly, 'How do you call yourself?'

How can we move on from this without doffing a purple cap to a musical legend? Were you similarly baffled by the controversy surrounding Prince? At points 'The Artist' and 'Symbol', and who was also called at one time 'The artist formerly known as Prince', he was born Prince Rogers Nelson. Prince Rogers had been named after his father's stage name. From what I remember, the name changes were due to issues with his music and its availability, but still, what a journey!

I think that monyms give you the opportunity to define yourself. I wouldn't be William Thompson, I'd be William, and then I'd be free to contextualise myself, or even allow others to do that on my behalf. William the Stoic, or William the Father, or William the Communicator. Although in the short term this would be a great marketing strategy, I'd lose who I was in the context of my most significant relationships, my forefathers and my children, which is why surnames are so important, as we'll see in this next section.

Surnames

How about surnames? Do they have any hold over our destiny? I remember sitting on a train trying to read when four guys got on and sat at the table next to me, behaving much as a pride of adolescent lions would. I felt like Sir David Attenborough as I studied them: back patting, barging, laughing, cajoling, pandering to each other. Lovers of horse racing, they were middle-aged men arguing over runners and riders displayed for them in a broadsheet newspaper, they were on their way to Cheltenham for the famous Gold Cup. It was almost as if they were hungrily sizing up their prey. The dominant male of the pride broke off to make a phone call – 'Hi, I'm just calling to confirm that my son is going to be able to attend football training tonight… Yes … His name is [redacted] Gamble'. I had to hide my amusement as I reached for my notebook. Mr Gamble was really engrossed in his gambling! Did he have any other choice though, or was he predisposed, as nominative determinists would say, to gambling because of his name?

It's generally recognised that surnames came from different sources and weren't common in Europe before the 12th century. A surname can evolve from a job: John who was a blacksmith was John the Smith, which became John Smith. These surnames could just as easily be Potter, Mason, or even Knight! It can evolve from a location (this is called toponymic); for example, Michelle who lived over by the lake was Michelle Lake, although she could have lived by a wood (Atwood) or perhaps she inspired Tolkien and had lived under a hill, potentially providing a pseudonym for a certain Hobbit bound to a perilous quest involving a dark lord, pipe weed and rings…

Surnames can be patronymic or matronymic. Patronymic is being named after the father; for example, where Peter had a dad called Jack, he was Peter Jackson. Matronymic would be where Peter would be named after his mum Megan and would quite possibly have been called Peter Megson. A fine chap, no doubt, and still with a flair for directing films, one would hope! Nicknames can also be a source of surnames. I love the film *The Three Amigos*, and one of the actors in it was Martin Short. One cannot get away from the undeniable fact that he is. His father was Short (certainly by name as I have found no dimensional records) and *Hello* magazine's biography of the actor reveals that he was a Catholic who had left Ireland during the Irish war of independence.[5] According to the Dictionary of American Family Names[6], Short is a nickname and comes from a Middle English word 'Schort'.

Clan names

It's fascinating to consider the implications of a name in the wider community. Clans are found in China, Poland, Mongolia, amongst the Xhosa tribe in Africa, and in Scotland. Scottish clans are groups of families based in close proximity who recognised and submitted to a clan chief.

> 'It is a common misconception that those who bear a clan surname are automatically descended from a clan chief. The ability of a clan to defend its territory from other clans depended greatly on attracting as many followers as possible. Being a member of a large and powerful clan became a distinct advantage in the lawless Highlands and followers might adopt the clan name to curry favour with the Laird, to show solidarity, for basic protection, or because their lands were taken by a more powerful neighbour, and they had little option. Yet others joined a clan on the promise of much-needed sustenance.'[7]

As soon as you become associated with a group of people and take their name, there is an orchestrated dynamic of service, support, and submission in return for a human being's greatest perceived needs:

provision and protection. Provision and protection are a human being's two biggest drivers and it's amazing how your name can unlock these in the hearts and minds of others, whether that's through the Oxbridge old boys' network, an American fraternity or a Scottish clan.

The Isle of Lewis is an incredible place, not least because it describes exactly what it is: an Isle of Lewises. The family name MacLeod means 'son of Lewis' and they're understandably everywhere. Kenneth MacLeod, grandson of Kenneth MacLeod, and owner of a butcher's shop in Stornoway on the Isle of Lewis established almost 100 years ago named 'MacLeod and MacLeod' shares about clans:

> 'I suspect that then it was more important, and the need for the protection of the clan was more important, but it's so different now. We are more individual now and have more of a responsibility to look after ourselves. The burden of provision and protection now lies on society and the individual rather than the clan. I think that this is a good thing, because as individuals we're not so reliant on a particular individual, because if you do look back at history, the masses were reliant on one or two individuals to make decisions for them. If you look back at Scottish history on its own, then if a clan chief called his clan to battle, they all jumped and ran to his assistance because they were under his protection. So, in that regard things have moved on and the individual is responsible for himself and his own rather than reliant on the handouts of one individual to whom he always seemed to be indebted. They lived on his land; they didn't own their own land. They worked for him, paid him his rent and then when he required their services, they were obliged to give them. Ultimately in many cases, give their lives to him. About 40% of the people I know are MacLeods. What's really prevalent is nicknames. People very often in these parts are not described by

their first name or surname, but by their nickname terminology. Even if you were to say John MacLeod of Barvis, well there are a lot of John MacLeods in Barvis, so to differentiate between them they may use a middle name, an abbreviation, or a nickname!'

Wee Kek Koon is a journalist and according to his article in the *South China Morning Post*, the Chinese had surnames way before Europeans decided it was time to try and distinguish between the fifteen Johns in the village. He wrote:

'Fortunately, when the first emperor of the Qin dynasty unified China into a centralised empire in 221BC, his administration standardised many aspects of everyday life, including names. The xing and shi names, which by then had become interchangeable in practical terms, were formally merged into the single concept of the family name. ... The earliest Chinese family names might have originated in a matrilineal society. Many of these earliest clan names, known as "Xing", carry the ideograph for "woman" (女), such as Ji (姬), Ying (嬴), Yao (姚), Jiang (姜) and so on, which are probably representative of an era between 5,000 and 6,000 years ago, when people knew who their mother was but would have been less sure of their father's identity. The word xing (姓) is made up of two ideographs that read "born of a woman", and a person's xing name placed them within a kinship group that forbade marriage between its members.'[8]

We're going to explore this further in the chapter on international cultural naming practices, where I share material from my interview with Kek Koon.

How a name choice can be influenced

Now that we have explored the heritage of names, let's look at how a name could influence the one who carries it and those who hear it.

In their paper about social and demographic influences on name choice, Bush, et al, explore naming trends. They come to this conclusion: 'Name choices in the UK appear simultaneously influenced both by external social forces (such as the varying cultural dominance of Christianity over time) and internal mechanisms (such as via the drift and preference models of cultural change).'[9]

We have a wider pool of names to choose from now than ever before in history! We read in social media about how given names are becoming increasingly diverse and creative. Statistics drawn from Galbi's research[10] reveal that since the beginning of the 19th century, popular UK names changed dramatically where in the year 1800, 24 per cent of girls were named Mary and 22 per cent of boys were John. Imagine being in a room with 100 ladies, and 24 of them were called Mary! In comparison, by 1994 the most popular girls name was Emily, shared by just over 3 per cent, and for boys it was James with just over 4 per cent.

Go popular

Surely the best way to come to a decision over a name is to find one that's really popular. Historian Theodor Mommsen reflects on two cultures when it comes to popularity guiding naming. One seemed to focus on simplicity and the popularity of a few strong names, while the other seemed less into popular names and more into freedom of expression: 'It seems as if the small and ever diminishing number and the meaningless character of the Italian, and particularly of the Roman, individual names, compared with the luxuriant and poetical fullness of those of the Greeks, were intended to illustrate the truth that it was characteristic of the one nation to reduce all to a level, of the other to promote the free development of personality.'[11]

Kessler et al write that 'the popularity of baby names was very robust until the end of the 18th century but since then names have become a matter of fashion, with a typical time evolution involving growth and decline'.[12] Their paper goes to great lengths to explore the ebb and flow of these trends and dynamics. The popularity of names flows and fluctuates massively from the raising of awareness to saturation and negative response. For example, when suddenly everyone is called Michelle, there's a response in some to think of something different.

Often the honouring of a significant individual will see a flourishing of babies named after them because it's a good name that's been drawn to people's attention. Examples of this include Socrates (either the Greek philosopher or the Brazilian football star), Oprah, and George. A figure from the entertainment industry or a name in a popular song can inspire a tsunami of 'Oh, that's a nice name!' A prime example of this is 'Madison' (the name of Daryl Hannah's mermaid character from the film *Splash* with Tom Hanks). US website Social Security Administration has a page dedicated to baby names,[13] which really is a great resource, and shows graphically how when the film came out in 1984, Madison wasn't even in the top 1000 most popular names. Thirteen years after the release of the film it was top ten, its meteoric climb resulting in its position in the top three for seven years. Why not have a look at the website and perhaps find out what the most popular name was in the year of your birth, or whether your name has ever been in the top 1000!

Go unpopular/kooky

Maybe trying to find something unique could be a considerable motivation for you in picking a name, so does an unusual name affect your job opportunities? In an interview called 'Racism in Football: Our Stories' that featured broadcaster and presenter Reshmin Chowdhury,[14] Reshmin says:

+'I 100 per cent, 100 million per cent feel that if I'd had an easier name, if my name wasn't Reshmin, if my name was Claire, I think that my journey would have been a lot easier. There's no two ways about it. People get really confused by 'Reshmin' and then 'Chowdhury'; it's just too many unfamiliar letters to say in one go.'

I found this on a 'GameSpot' forum discussion on naming[15]:
Contributor 1: 'Being kooky for the sake of kooky isn't individuality. It's called being Zooey Deschanel in any movie she's been in.'
Contributor 2: 'The act of being kooky is not what I'm referring to. It's deciding your own name, rather than going by what others have decided to name you. Where I live, half the women are named Ashley. Totally serious. And two-thirds of the girls I dated were named Ashley. And they usually hate that they share their name with so many others. It's boring. If we chose our own names, there might be more diversity… right now, I happen to be wearing a t-shirt bearing a triforce symbol. That says something about me. I'm a gamer. More notably, I enjoy The Legend of Zelda games. My name, however, does not. My name's Darren. That tells you nothing about me. Your name means nothing. Literally nothing. It's your actions that define you.'
I tried to find a way of reaching out to Darren, but no joy. I would have liked to send him a copy of this book!

Better name, better life?

So, whether the name is popular or rare, what should really matter is whether it will help you become successful. Shouldn't it? Can your name on its own change anything? Can it open doors or close them? Because if so, surely every namer has a moral duty to ensure that the name of their child opens as many doors to opportunity as possible, or at the very least not shut any.

There really should be a table of some sort that reveals the names that will ensure that your child gets the best education or job or enjoys the best relationships. This is a field of questioning that the prestigiously heralded (others would say irreverently unorthodox) economist, Stephen Levitt, decided to explore. In their groundbreaking book *Freakonomics*[16], Levitt and Dubner set out on a mission in which 'a rogue economist explores the hidden side of everything'.

In the chapter entitled 'Perfect Parenting, Part II; or: Would a Roshinda by any other name smell so sweet?' opens with a story about parents who named their baby son 'Winner' and three years later their seventh and final child, a boy they chose to name 'Loser'. We are given an overview of these boys' journeys. One son became really successful (as far as society's judgement is concerned), while the other one careered through a life marked with challenges and seemingly controversial choices. Can you guess which one is which though? Loser thrived within the New York Police Department becoming Detective and then Sergeant (despite people generally feeling uncomfortable with his name, often abbreviating it or avoiding it altogether through using a nickname) while desperately and ironically, Winner Lane's criminal record reflected nearly three dozen arrests.

The next questions raised in the chapter relate to the correlation between the name given to a baby and the parent's socioeconomic status. They reveal that 'considering the relationship between income and names and given the fact that income and education are strongly correlated, it is not surprising to find a similarly strong link between the parents' level of education and the name they give their baby.' Fascinating insights are expressed as they list the most common income related names, what they describe as 'high-end' and 'low-end' for boys and girls, before progressing onto the comparative education level of the parents, 'high-end' parents and 'low-end' parents amongst the same groups of children. The results are shown in Figure 1.

The focus of this section is to see whether rich, well-educated people who choose what they determine to be potentially successful names for their children are right, so let's see how these names hold up to the 2020 rich list. Surely the top ten will all be called Alexandra, Katherine, or Benjamin?

Top ten on Forbes' World's Billionaires List:[17]

1. Larry, 2. Mark, 3. Larry, 4. Sergey, 5. Elon, 6. Laurene, 7. Donald, 8. Eric, 9. Gordon, 10. Jan.

Where are the supposed successful names in the billionaires list? No one in this top ten rich list has these names, which shows that success is not just about your name.

	Most Common Names, 'High end'				
	1	2	3	4	5
High income parents – girls	Alexandra	Lauren	Katherine	Madison	Rachel
High income parents – boys	Benjamin	Samuel	Jonathan	Alexander	Andrew
High education parents – girls	Katherine	Emma	Alexandra	Julia	Rachel
High education parents – boys	Benjamin	Samuel	Alexander	John	William

Figure 1: So-called 'high-end' names

Back to Levitt, whose research and analysis goes on to suggest that 'once a name catches on among high-income, highly educated parents, it starts working its way down the socioeconomic ladder.' In other words, it becomes popular. They also explore research done by Roland G Fryer Jr, a young economist who wanted to explore whether distinctive black culture was the cause or the reflection of the economic disparity between black and white people. He sums up his research by saying that 'On average, a person with a distinctively black name – whether it is a woman named Imani or a man named DeShawn – does have a worse life outcome than a woman named Molly, or a man named Jake. But it isn't the fault of their names.' This illustrates the difference between causality and correlation. An individual doesn't get into university because of her name (causality), but there are many girls with her name that do get into university (correlation).

Levitt's conclusion in light of the data explored is that a vast proportion of parents use this opportunity to give a name as a way to 'signal their own expectations of how successful their child will be. The name isn't likely to make a shard of difference. But the parents can at least feel better knowing that, from the very outset, they tried their best'.

This field of study had also piqued the interest of Albert Mehrabian. For his book *The Name Game*,[18] he surveyed 1,800 people in the early 90s. He rated their first names for success, morality, warmth, health, and masculinity/femininity, in order to give 'new parents an idea about the impression their babies' names make on others'. His conclusions about these categories are illustrated in Figure 2.

Top 10 girl names that connote a successful person

1	2	3	4	5	6	7	8	9	10
Jacqueline	Morgan	Elizabeth	Katherine	Victoria	Lauraine	Susan	Catherine	Kate	Madeleine

Top 10 girl names that connote failure

1	2	3	4	5	6	7	8	9	10
Wilma	Weeza	Virgie	Trixie	Tina	Swoosie	Suzee	Soosie	Sissy	Mush

Top 10 boy names that connote a successful person

1	2	3	4	5	6	7	8	9	10
Steven	Ross	Christopher	James	Robert	David	Kenneth	Parker	Thomas	Madison

Top 10 boy names that connote failure

1	2	3	4	5	6	7	8	9	10
Rufus	Rude	Butch	Angel	Alfie	Garee	Normee	Bud	Petie	Phonso

Figure 2: Mehrabian's top ten names

Again, note that none of these supposed successful names appear in Forbes' top ten rich list. The number of syllables seems important. With the girls, the average number of syllables in a name that would connote a successful person is 2.7, the names that connote failure almost all had two syllables, which made them sound easier and more melodic.

A 2015 article titled '25 Baby Names That Spell Career Success'[19] triumphantly reports that in first place we have John, and in second, Mary. The caveat is that both names were incredibly popular 55 years before that research was undertaken. The article concludes: 'There were 4,698 executives named John in the U.S. in 2014. This March, *The New York Times* published a slightly distressing article titled, "Fewer Women Run Big Companies Than Men Named John."'[20] The research for this article was based on an Ernst & Young report on women on US boards; however, 'John' also doesn't appear in Forbes' top ten rich list...

After conducting extensive research into extensive research, there is nothing conclusive here that proves the name is the prime cause of an individual's success. (However, this begs the question, what constitutes success?) Naming trends seem to reflect the parents' need for significance more than anything else. In certain cases, names seem to help a child move through life more freely or conversely, cause them to carry a heavy burden.

Maybe a name is what you make it

How you live your life can have a direct impact on the way people respond to your name in the future. LM Montgomery wrote this in *Anne of Avonlea* (the sequel to *Anne of Green Gables*): '"That's a lovely idea, Diana," said Anne enthusiastically. "Living so that you beautify your name, even if it wasn't beautiful to begin with… making it stand in people's thoughts for something so lovely and pleasant that they never think of it by itself."'[21]

I remember conversations in the school staff room while a teacher, hearing staff talking of certain names with dread. 'Oh, he's a _____ (insert prejudiced name here) _____ they are always awful, every _____

I've ever met has been horrible.' In Stewart Perrie's article, 'Teachers and Parents Reveal Kids' Names Linked With Best And Worst Behaviour'[22] he shares a survey conducted in the UK by My Nametags and Censuswide (an international market research consultancy headquartered in London). They asked 1,500 teachers, parents and kids which names they identified with good and bad behaviour. Those surveyed matched the names Jack, Harry, Charlie, Oliver, and George with the naughtiest boys, while Mia, Ella, Isabella, Amelia and Sophia topped the equivalent list for the naughtiest girls. Is it possible that every Ella is going to be a tearaway? Of course not, but prejudice makes life easier, doesn't it? We don't have to go to all the trouble of getting to know someone before deciding if we can like or respect them; just simply 'judge beforehand' (the etymological underpinning of the word prejudice), which then takes us perfectly back to what Anne said, that we could each live in a way that 'beautified' our name in the minds of others while at the same time determining to move as far away from prejudice as we are able. Surely it's the namer's responsibility to consider these things. If, however, you believe that a name can be beautified, that you have the confidence to give people reason to change their opinion of a name because you carry it, then you are owning your identity beyond others' perceptions and perhaps making up for your namer's faux pas.

Names, gender, and employability

Grace Jennings-Edquist raises some compelling questions in an article titled 'Why parents are choosing "masculine" names for their baby girls'[23] Could a more 'masculine' name give a female more opportunity in a male-dominated world? Grace had been interviewing Kimberley Linco, a social researcher at the Australian social research company McCrindle, who told her, 'We're coming into this world of breaking down gender stereotypes, and our opinion is that parents are opting to not box their child in with a feminine-sounding name'. Their research revealed a significant increase in names such as Billie, Frankie and Harper. In 2017 Harper was the 10th most popular name in Australia; back in 2014 it was

24th. Grace had also connected with Michelle Brady, a senior research fellow in sociology at the University of Queensland's School of Social Science who told her, 'There's research showing that [the gender-neutral name trend] may actually pay off,' and also referred to a US study that explored whether masculine names help female lawyers become judges.

Termed the 'Portia Hypothesis', the study conducted by Coffey and McLaughlin provided the 'first empirical test of the Portia Hypothesis', thus successfully demonstrating a correlation between females with masculine monikers and a more successful legal career.[24] This awareness and line of thinking is reflected in society as we see trends of girls being given more masculine names. Of course, the question then is whether this is because parents are keen for their girls to have more confidence in a male-orientated world, or in case their daughter decides to question their very gender in the future. Children born since 2010 are referred to as 'Generation Alpha', the name coined by Generational researcher Mark McCrindle himself after an online survey in 2008. Gender roles, the #MeToo movement and discussions over gender fluidity will clearly be a significant part of their societal backdrop, so why not future proof their name? In the celebrity world, Blake Lively and Ryan Reynolds wanted to name their firstborn after Ryan's father. Their daughter was subsequently named James, and in an interview with People Magazine, Lively said 'Right now, my daughter thinks there's no difference between her and a boy. She can do anything he can do ... She has every opportunity that he has'.[25] From the other perspective, tables showing the most popular names for boys don't indicate a trend towards their names becoming more feminine. Research into this area is scarce and certainly calls for further exploration.

Research clearly shows that there is a gender bias in job application, so maybe giving a child a name that is more gender neutral would be of benefit. In their paper 'An Experimental Investigation of Sexual Discrimination in Hiring in the English Labor Market', Riach and Rich found that

> 'In the two 'mixed occupations' there was statistically significant discrimination against men. Men

encountered discrimination four times more often than women in analyst programming, and three and a half times more often than women in chartered accounting when it came to the serious business of interviewing, rather than the mechanical process of dispatching application forms. When training firms issued invitations to interview, men were denied interviews on 60% of those occasions, while women were so denied at a rate of only 17%. Men were denied interviews at a rate of 47% in analyst programming, compared with 12% for women. In the 'male-dominated' occupation of engineering, women encountered discrimination at twice the male rate; women were rejected for interview on 46% of the occasions when invitations were issued, compared with a male rate of 23%. In the 'female-dominated' occupation of secretary men encountered discrimination at almost four times the female rate; men were rejected for interview on 59% of the occasions when invitations were issued, compared with a female rate of 16%.'[26]

Smith et al's summary in *The Name Game* concludes, 'Practical implications for applicants (for various roles) include the fact that much more information is revealed in a person's name than would first seem likely. Perhaps applicants should consider using their first initials rather than a full first name.'[27]

What's the solution, then? How can we choose a name for a child when we have no idea the role that they will apply for in the future? What if the field of ability they flourish in doesn't even exist yet? If everyone had the same name, surely this would force employers to look beyond the label to the real nature of the individual. Of course, this line of thought feels absurd, and we will discover why over the next chapters.

In 1977 Richard L Zweingenhaft in his article 'The Other Side of Unusual First Names' explored several ideas: 'Although a number of studies have indicated that having an unusual first name has a deleterious effect on the individual, it was hypothesized that under certain conditions this would not be the case.' He undertook several studies. One of the studies found that 'unusual named members of the upper class were more, not less, likely to be found in *Who's Who*'. Another of his studies explored data accrued from over 10,000 high school students from North Carolina, highlighted the 'importance of considering the socioeconomic class, race, and sex of the individual before generalizing about the impact of an unusual first name. Though the patterns differed, none of the four subgroups studied – white males, white females, black males, and black females – showed consistent negative effects from having unusual names'.[28]

How has this stimulated your thinking? Were you aware of the minefield of choices your namer navigated?

Do you actively beautify your name, or do you hope that people see you beyond your name? And do you extend that grace to others or do you prejudge others because of their name?

***

Hopefully having read this chapter you will feel more able to make a considered decision if you are ever called upon to be a namer. Maybe you won't. Perhaps you will feel vindicated and even more resolute in your commitment to name a child Matthew. I can testify to many stories of namers who have taken one look at the child and called them something that had not previously been anywhere on the naming list.

Maybe this chapter has encouraged you to think more deeply about your name, where it came from and how it connects you to history. Maybe one of your ancestors was a Cook, a King, or a Carpenter? Is it wrong to want more from a name, to want it to open doors or inspire those who hear it? I have shown you research to equip you to consider the nature versus nurture debate in relation to names. Do you believe that giving a child a particular name will ensure their prosperity? If you believe that the decision can be influenced by exploring the future, should we not also consider the past? This is what our next chapter explores, because if you give a name, it tells the recipient a lot about you.

Interviews

The next chapter explores how individuals can receive or reject their name. I think that when exploring these ideas, it's crucial to gain insight from the stories of others, in order to really start asking yourself how the material could be significant for you.

The first of two interviews is with Befrin, a multilingual actor, singer and songwriter who is based in Sydney, Australia. Befrin's interest in humanitarianism, animal rights and healthy self-development, as you can see throughout the interview, is rooted in her life journey.

The second is with Gary, who I have known for many years as a business mentor, a gatekeeper, and a visionary. The story he shares in his interview provides an enlightening insight into the joy of discovering yourself and your family through your name.

Befrin

'My mother was the wife of a refugee. My father was welcomed into Sweden on a humanitarian visa, my mum followed about a year later and they married there. A few months later, she realised she was pregnant. When she first found out that she was pregnant she opened up the balcony doors and walked out onto the balcony. It was morning, and the early morning breeze hit her; that was the first thing that she experienced having had this news and straightaway something in her said this is a girl, this is a daughter and she's going to be named Serwa, which means "morning breeze" in Kurdish.

Throughout her pregnancy they referred to this baby that was coming as Serwa and it kind of went without saying that this was my name. My mum's Swedish wasn't great yet, whereas my dad had learned to master the alphabet, so he was the one filling out

Why Does Your Name Matter?

the paperwork and filled out names. A few weeks later my mum received a birth certificate in the mail, and there was my name – Befrin. That was a bit of a shock to her because that wasn't a name that they had discussed at all, and yet, that was my official name. She asked him about it and his response was, "Do you really think that I would allow you to choose the name of this baby?" My mum is very stubborn though, she was 16 or 17 years old when the Islamic Revolution took place in Iran. Overnight she was forced to separate from all the male friends that she played with. She had to change schools to an all-female school and had to cover up. That was one thing that she absolutely could not understand, why suddenly out of nowhere she had to cover her hair. During one of the first few days of school there was a piece of hair showing under her hijab. One of her teachers called her prostitute for it. As a result, she actually ripped the hijab off her head, threw it on the ground and walked home without it. That evening she was visited by soldiers, they usually come at night. They ripped her out of bed and locked her up; she was jailed for nine months for that. So she continued to call me Serwa, and she still does 30 years on, so he calls me Serwa as well.

In official settings and especially Swedish settings my name is and was Befrin. In school I grew up being called Befrin. I eventually translated it into being Serwa as my Kurdish name and Befrin as my Swedish, or official, name. Throughout my upbringing it almost became as though there was this Serwa personality that was my Kurdish personality. All my Kurdish friends knew me as Serwa, and so I acted in a culturally appropriate way when around these Kurdish friends, I behaved as Serwa. Whereas Befrin was, for want of a better term, my white personality almost. As somebody that is dark, I had this want and urge to be as white as possible to fit in into this world that I was being brought up in. Although Befrin isn't really a Swedish name it sounded more Swedish than Serwa and it was what I preferred using.

Befrin is Kurdish for Snow White. It's strange, I can relate to that name a lot. Snow White was very sensitive and friends with all the animals and that was something I definitely became, so it did fit a little bit. Just like Snow White I was born very pale with black, black hair and very red lips, according to my dad.

So, when I model or put myself across for work I introduce myself as Befrin, because it's my white name. Everyone in the white world I am Befrin to, and that's how I feel most comfortable. Whereas, when I'm hanging out with parts of our large Kurdish community in Australia, going to Newroz celebrations [Newroz is the Kurdish celebration of spring and celebration of freedom and strength of the people] or whatever; it's natural for me to call myself Serwa. It's interesting because it's the same for my mum as well. When she speaks to other white people about me, she refers to me as Befrin to avoid confusion. When she was talking to authorities or making appointments for me when I was a child, she would call me Befrin, because that was my official name. So it's natural for me, I was born into this duality of these two names. There's also no doubt in my mind that if I ever went back to Kurdish Iran, I would never call myself Befrin, even though that is a Kurdish name.

It's very hard to explain something that you've never really questioned before; this is just how I was brought up, and yet there is this difference between the two. What I find more fascinating, which is something that I've picked up on as I've grown older and developed a stronger sense of myself, is just how different I am based on which of these two names I am. Serwa is the very sort of traditional kind of personality, almost. I try to be as proper as I can, and I fall into the cultural stereotypes. So, when there are guests Serwa will make the tea and Serwa will serve the sweets and be very traditional.

When I think of Serwa I really see this calm, nurturing, mellow kind of sweet soul. Whereas when I'm Befrin that's a more creative, spontaneous, rebellious self. The self where I don't have to control or try to stay in line to not offend. I have no idea why it's become that way, but it's definitely two separate personalities. That sounds really mad, it's not that intense; but I definitely sort of adapt the way I am based on what setting I'm in. If you want to call it White versus Kurdish or Befrin versus Serwa I don't know, but it's definitely two different ways of being for me.'

Gary

'I am from a lovely family, but a difficult family. I was born in Leaf, what you would describe as a slum in Edinburgh. In some parts it's gentrified, it's gone upmarket, but when I was a boy, it was the home to the dockers, to rough, manly men and working women bleaching the steps. Hard men, bringing the money in after they'd had a pint in the many local bars of Leaf. My dad had a variety of jobs, working in a brewery, a bus conductor, a bus driver and later in life, working for a catering company. From the age of three and a half up till the age of 11 I was in and out of care, because my mother couldn't cope and then also because my brother was disabled. Everybody blamed my mother that he was disabled, they thought it was alcohol, they thought it was cigarettes but of course it wasn't any of these, it was thalidomide, (at that time) nobody knew what had caused it.

Kind of lacking an identity, lacking an understanding of who my family was, these things didn't appear to impact me, but behind the scenes I was in and out of care with my auntie Sandra, my mother's cousin. You can imagine as I was growing up, that I was torn between families and attended many different primary schools. I was with my auntie Sandra for some of the time and imposed care through social services the rest of the time. When I was with Auntie Sandra, I really enjoyed it. She had parties and drank and played Elvis's music all the time. I really enjoyed it. I never got hugged by my mother or my father. I never had fun with my family, they were distracted by this disabled child. The need to know about yourself more was strong for me, because I didn't know too much about myself.

During the year I turned 42, my dad and mum died. I did the eulogies for both and at the end of my mum's, my auntie Einar said to me, "You know, you're an orphan now, what are you going to do with your life? Who are you?" I said to myself, "Wow, I'm an orphan." I hadn't realised. She said, "What mark are you going to make with your life? Everyone's going to look at you now as the oldest in the family." Auntie Einar got out her little black metal box, like a petty cash tin with a little key. She took it out from under the TV and put it in front of me, opened it almost like a treasure chest, or Pandora's box. "Have you seen this?" I hadn't, it was a photograph of my mum and dad's wedding group. "This is your auntie Peggy, and this is your great granny Betty." She knew so much about my family, and I knew nothing. "Why don't you go and try and find out who these people are, if you can?" So, I came back to Liverpool and over the years I started researching the family tree through *Ancestry* and *ScotlandsPeople*. There's a hugely emotional connection you get to the families that you never actually met and that's what research does to you; it connects you. A son is born, a son gets married. That son has 13 children, 11 of them die through smallpox, cholera, and diseases of that age and you think, what would have been, what would have happened if they lived?

My mother always said to me, before she died, that it would be wonderful if I could find her mum, because she had abandoned her and she wanted to know where she was. I remember her telling me in the 70s that all she knew about her mother was that she came from Kirkcaldy. That's all she knew. Ancestry and Scotland's people have kind of done two things. It's made my life more whole because it's actually allowed me to join up all the dots and fill in all the gaps, to a point. But there's a dangerous side to in in that. It's quite addictive. The only common denominator between you and your past is your name. Usually it's just your surname, your first name doesn't really matter, except when it passes down. That's my common denominator, all the way through history. Those are the only ways that I could find people. The only way I could find them was through on birth certificates and death certificates. After much research [Gary's husband] Stephen said, 'Stop playing around with Egypt, Rome, Constantinople, Cornwall, Wales and centurions. Come back to reality and find the most important part of your mother's identity and your identity'. Well, you know, 24 hours later I found her and subsequently my Uncle William. My mum had died, but I went and met Uncle William.

My family tree, the events of 2002, them dying… is why I became a councillor, and an elected member. It's how I became Lord Mayor; Auntie Einar saying to me, "What difference are you going to make?". I kind of changed into this. I created two charities in Liverpool… it was no longer about wealth ambition. Everybody wants to be wealthy, have a nice home, nice holidays, but actually it was about people. Doing my family tree was about me as an individual, but doing my charity work was actually a reminder of her.

That's where family trees and history lead you, to feel more of a connection with the past you may never have known you had. Now I'm helping other people do genealogy research, do their family tree, to find out information using these devices in a matter of minutes or hours. It used to have been impossible to find a lost grandmother, but to find these things, then actually see history and realise that you're part of that history, a small bit player mind you, is incredible.

I mentioned Auntie Einar's story. Her story started me on this trajectory, to find out who I am. I think when you're younger it's not that important, you're too busy living life. As you get older you start to understand people die, you kind of accept your own mortality. So, before you die what's better than actually finding out your family's past. Your legacy in terms of your only legacy that you have a personal connection to. It's understanding your maker and the routes that they've taken that you should be proud of. Whether that's becoming somebody who collects and empties

> bins, or becomes a major scientist and wins a Nobel Prize. We're all equally important, but until you start to question your Auntie Einars, your Garys, your Williams and have the conversation, it's lost. It's the conversations where you see the whites of somebody's eyes, and you hear a passion in their voice, and the soul in their heart of what makes them who they are. I want to know more. I want to explore.'

5

To Receive a Name

A formless rushing ahead, indiscriminate severing of the roots of the past, results in emptiness, a lack of presence, and thus, also, a lack of future.

Paul Tillich[1]

Your name matters because it gives you an insight to how you feel about your namer. Have you received your name? Taken it with both hands and owned it? The insight your name gives you into your relationship with your namer is, but also possibly isn't, a good thing for you.

Your name connects you to others. A name usually comes from the primary 'others' with whom most of us begin life, and could be our birth parent(s), our adoptive parent(s), the staff at the hospital or those at the social care provision. A name, then, is the gift of a namer or namers. This gift was a connection to their past, their present and/or an insight into their heart for your future.

In the previous chapter we examined some of the research around names, where they come from, what they may or may not do for you or say about you – all of which is very external. This chapter will go internal. Your name reflects who you are, but it also reflects your community because it came from them. This is the dichotomy within a name: on one hand, it identifies you as an individual, while at the same time, it connects you to your community. You are a link in a chain of humanity and your name places you in that chain. This understanding strengthens you and also strengthens the chain. David Patterson put it like this:

'But what indeed do we know when we know our name? To know our name is to know the names of those who confer a name upon us, the names of our mother and our father. It means knowing a tradition borne by those who have borne our names before us; it means knowing a teaching that harbours our future and our mission in life, as inscribed in our name; it means recognising that we are called by name and must answer to our name.'[2]

This is my challenge to you: consider as you go through this chapter the extent to which you are reconciled to your name. Consider if this reflects the extent to which you are reconciled to your namer. We will explore this dynamic through this chapter and I hope that by the end of it you will be comfortable with the extent to which you receive your name and the extent to which you are reconciled with your namer and those who have gone before you.

**

How can you receive your name with assuredness if so many others have the same name? Josh Swain from Arizona decided that there were too many people called Josh. He decided that there should be a fight to gain the honour of being the *one* Josh. He organised a fight to the death – well, they were fighting with swimming noodles, so there was actually more risk of someone dying of laughter. The winner was, unsurprisingly, Josh. It doesn't matter how many people called Josh there are; each one of you is uniquely named, because the context of your naming is as unique as you are. Your name is the key to you as an individual, but it's also a key to you in society and community, because the building blocks of communities tend to be families. Your name can be a bridge that connects you to the heart of your namer. What did they draw from? What was their dream for the future, and (if this is important), how can you discover this? Have you had this conversation with those you have named? This is a tool for reconciliation and remembrance.

Avoiding binary thinking

Which of these statements resonate with you more profoundly?

- You are an individual, you are not just one of a faceless mass of humanity.
- You are not your own entity; you are one of infinite expressions of humanity.

An either-or approach is often unhelpful. Let me illustrate this; I am in the throes of a mixer tap revolution. Up until quite recently, I would turn the tap so that only hot water came out, being careful of the scalding water until turning the handle to the extreme cold side, adding water until it reached just the right temperature to wash my dishes. Now I've started to move the handle to a more central point and allow warm water at just the right temperature to come out.

I believe in truth and in right and wrong. However, it's not always helpful to assume that life can be neatly divided into right or wrong. Why do we tend to do this? Does this tendency reflect our laziness or our desire to control? Or is it simply that what's in between – grey – is too ambiguous? I hate grey; it's nondescript, murky, shifting. Then I had a revelation. If black is the absence of light and white is full light, then what's in between them isn't grey at all, it's a rainbow! (Cue rolling of eyes.) Hear me out. I'm not talking daisy chains, unicorns and a short, red-headed guy in a green jacket looking for a pot of gold; I'm talking about seeing beauty and value in the effervescent spectrum of a third way.

I have struggled with black and white thinking in many ways but I'm seeing things differently as I grow older and mellow out. There are many examples of black and white thinking – my way/your way, politically left/politically right, introvert/extrovert, can cook/can't cook, can play sport/can't play sport, is intelligent/isn't intelligent, and then the one that we are going to focus on in this chapter: you and your name are your identity as an individual, and as part of a community.

We are individuals, but we're not just individuals

'My name is my business, it's up to me what I do with it, if I adapt it, switch it or change it. I'm my own person and can do what I like.' Do you agree or disagree? Maybe thinking about the diversity of snowflakes will help.

What an extraordinary expression of individuality snowflakes are. Apparently a trillion snowflakes fall annually and each one is unique. How does that stack up against us as humans? The Population Research Bureau estimates that up until 2021 there have been 117 billion humans on our planet so far.[3] We, like snowflakes, must be a pretty diverse bunch if there has never been a single replication. So yes. You are created as a unique individual, and with a desire to be more than just an individual.

I have a Wilson volleyball with a picture of face on it in the shape of a hand. I have it for two reasons. Firstly, because I've enjoyed playing volleyball since college, and second, because it reminds me of a poignant scene in *Castaway*. Plagued with extreme loneliness, Chuck, played by Tom Hanks, strikes up a relationship with a Wilson volleyball that he names Wilson. I remember watching the loss of this inanimate comrade towards the end of the film as it fell into the ocean and floated off. Chuck's anguished cries rang in my ears as tears rolled down my face. How ridiculous; it's a volleyball, yet after visiting Chuck's Island in Thailand I bought the replica to remind me of the innate desire of humans to exist in relationship.

Wilson exemplifies anthropomorphism: when we give human characteristics to things other than humans. I wrote in an earlier chapter about how we name things, but this idea takes it deeper. 'Anthropomorphism is a motivated process reflecting the active search for potential sources of connection.'[4] As demonstrated by Chuck, when we are lonely, we more readily relate with things that aren't human because the human is, as Aristotle said, 'a social animal'.[5] We need to be with others, community is about being with and Chuck created community through bringing life to a volleyball, giving it a name, talking to it, taking it everywhere with him and grieving terribly its loss.

We are individuals, but we function better in relationship, irrespective of where we are along the introvert/ extrovert spectrum. I experienced periods of intense loneliness over a particular period of my life when I had lost a significant relationship. Forcing myself to find and invest in new healthy relationships was key to my sanity. I remember being confronted by the stark truth of a lifetime of this particular pain while walking along Stanley Street in Liverpool. There is a bronze there of Eleanor Rigby, the subject of a mournful ballad by The Beatles. It beautifully describes the emptiness of a lonely death with no hope of being remembered or celebrated, her name was buried just as she was. It's good to take time to be alone, to be in nature, to be silent, to pray or to meditate because it enables us to really live the present, but prolonged alone-ness is detrimental. Receiving your name is easier when you are used to receiving other things that you are surrounded by, the sounds of family, the stillness of a lake, the busyness of the station… what is being given to you in that moment? Mindfulness is heralded for its positive impact on mental health and is derived from sati, the Buddhist teaching of existing in the present.[6] In Buddhism, the end goal is nirvana, so although I recognise the research showing its benefits, I'm wary of the idea of being so one with yourself that you are separate and devoid of everything else, even relationships. My friend Theodore Brun pointed out, 'Contrast this with the vision of heaven, where there is unity in diversity: every individuality of a person is retained, but so too is their place in the perfection of community – perfect relationships with God and with each other'. The far-reaching implications of Covid on our global and societal health are yet to become manifest, but months and months of isolation and loneliness will have caused real harm. The research that will be carried out and the results that will be elicited will, I have no doubt, be staggering. Addictions to alcohol, coffee, TV, and other stimulants will have rocketed because people will be yearning for a replacement for the stimulation that comes from interaction. Our commitment to fitness, both physical and mental, as well as our diet, will have been tested. The painful loss of loved ones, together with the bleak inability to freely mourn their passing, will grieve many for a significant period. You are a wonderfully fashioned individual; you are enough but you're also not enough. Your name is your name, it's you and it's yours, but it's also not, it's connected to others, just as you are.

We are part of a community, but we're not just part of a community

'I am not my own, I have become part of a whole that I have to submit to in every way. I no longer have free will or my own choices, I must submit to the leading of the one who has power over me.' No one really thinks like this, do they? You'd be surprised.

Should we throw ourselves wholeheartedly into community at the expense of individuality? Your name is your connection to your namer, and your family, but you aren't owned because of it, it's not a chain that holds you prisoner to an institution. No. There are very real and incredibly sad examples of situations where people have surrendered their all to a political party or an extreme community and in the process lost, and often been encouraged to lose, themselves. In the 1990s, Paul was part of our friendship group when Nirvana released their album *Nevermind*. In those days, before MTV had really caught on, a band crept up on you far more slowly than these days when bands really explode through social media. Songs people were singing would slowly become more familiar and you'd see more and more people wearing the same T-shirts, particularly the one with an underwater baby reaching out for money. Always into his music, Paul's enjoyment of it became more obsessive after Kurt Cobain's tragic death. He had already started wearing clothes worn by the ever-growing clique and I remember him increasingly distancing himself. I lost track of him as he got dragged into messing with drugs. As I look back it was almost as if he got swallowed by the culture of the people he was spending time with. Maybe we gave up on him. There is an intensity in losing oneself to a community that I've seen – the clothes, then the hair, the language. It almost works like a whirlpool – what was at first a naïve and gentle change in direction and focus accelerates unwittingly. The closer you get to the centre, the stronger the pull and the harder it is to escape. This happens to all of us to varying degrees online and with social media, when we find our opinion backed up by others to the exclusion of safe and necessary debate. One of the biggest problems with being exclusively community-focused is the echo chamber effect, in which all you hear is confirmation of what you're thinking.

The crucial issue here is that our identity isn't just found in the self, and it isn't just found in others; there is the potential for abuse in both of these extremes. Your name isn't just yours, it's also a connection to others, but it's not a chain, it's a held hand. You can hold the power, or you can allow someone else to wield power over you, or you can find the third way where there is a trust and love in the relationship. This is the key. Is there a reconciliation that needs to take place with your namer? Walking in your name and discovering your identity is and isn't something for you to do on your own. It's your responsibility and it's our responsibility. The last interview Jim Morrison gave was to Ben Fong-Torres, an editor of *Rolling Stone* magazine. The impact of Jim's band The Doors had been staggering. At the point of the interview, their fame was waning. Morrison is quoted as saying: 'Each generation wants new names, new symbols, new cycles.'[7] He is proven right across tribe and tongue. This is the curse of a breakdown in intergenerational relationships, that the new generation wants to 'divorce itself from its predecessors', to discover themselves for themselves. However, this leads to frustration and unproductivity. We are supposed to stand on the shoulders of those who have gone before us, not reject them and endlessly remake the wheel.

***

The two interviews prefacing this chapter point to how a name connects you and strengthens your sense of identity. Gary had crafted his identity through the work of his hands, both for himself and his siblings, but there was something missing. It was Gary's surname and the inspiration of a relative that opened the doors to reconciliation, and connection with a family that he had grown up without. The story of Befrin's identity journey is rooted in the exploration of her given names – a more intimate dance with her mother and father as individuals and as a couple as well as her cultural heritage and traditions. To receive a name is primarily to recognise the balance between our individuality and our communality. Then it's to see how it places us in the expanse of history. When you receive your name and are reconciled to who you are in relation to your predecessors, you allow yourself to be placed in the flow of history and time itself.

The tension of time – past, present, and future

Humans have always been entranced by the mystery of time. I experienced this in Fiji when I set out for my lookout spot before 4.00am. The Fijian archipelago is cut through by the 180th degree meridian line and just east of it is the International Date Line. I was going to be one of the first people in the entire world to welcome the first rays of light on Monday 18th October 2004. It was worth it. I was mesmerised as the first fingers of dawn reached out to me and then raced past to an expectant humanity.

It's this yearning to be able to somehow touch the start of something that had intrigued me about the Roman god Janus when, as a teenager, I was captivated by Roman and Greek mythology. Depicted with two heads, one looking forward, one back, he was worshipped in antiquity as the god of new beginnings, transitions, gateways, and the propagator of humanity. Stepping into something new is always done best having reflected on what's been before; this is the tension of the already and the not yet. It's impossible to adequately express the miracle of a new life, but it is a baton carrier. History is a depiction of the seamless transition of life to life, and a name can be an aid to seeing this.

Names mean something; they represent a place, a person, a song. However, at the deepest level they carry something; something intangible, a power that can have significant implications on the hearer.

How do we see ourselves as part of time, of an overarching historical narrative? You are not a solitary generation but a link in a chain, a carrier of a baton. However, for me to say, 'I am William Thompson, son of Andrew Thompson, son of Henry Thompson,' this would have negligible impact in my day-to-day relationships. Even if I went for a job interview, this would not ingratiate me to my prospective employers. In fact, an employer may consider that I was leaning on the success of my forebears to gain favour. This is a tragedy in our individualistic society. Hearing about someone getting a role 'because their father was part of the company' can incite cries of nepotism. In some cases, people get opportunities we don't believe they deserve because of this, but not always. I'm of the opinion that the idea of building upon the legacy of our forebears rather than every generation having to recreate the wheel has real value. I believe that this goes back to the issue of fathering and the loss of fathers in our society. Chapter six throws more light on how this position is reflected in cultures around the world, but for the time being, let me share with you a fascinating piece of writing from an Islamic text which I visited a mosque to get clarification on:

> 'In Sunan Abu Dawud [which I learnt is one of the six "canonical" hadith collections recognised by Sunni Muslims], it is narrated with a jayyid isnad from Abu'l-Darda' [this means that the text is recognised as having weight] that The Messenger of Allah (ىلص الله هيلع و سلم) ["Peace be upon him" in Arabic] said: "You will be called on the Day of Resurrection by your names and the names of your fathers, so choose good names for yourselves".'[8]

Why do the names of your forebears matter? In a world where we have an increasing mandate to 'find ourselves' and 'make our mark' we are in danger of letting go of the very rope that would lead us to a greater understanding of what 'our mark' would mean for us. In a society where religious and cultural institutions are being eroded, decried, vilified, and forgotten, I believe that we are abandoning firm foundations for waters of shifting tides and currents.

Is it time for you to explore your roots and ask questions that only your forebears could answer? Questions like: Who am I in your eyes? What was your heart for me as a child? Why do we stand for this? Why did we reject that? What was in your heart when you gave me this name? Which ultimately returns us to two key questions: 'Who are you, and who am I to you?'

What was in the heart of the giver when the gift was given?

In a lecture titled, 'Family as Foundational for a Relational Society', Dr Michael Schluter CBE said, 'The more you understand about your parents [or your namer] and their lifetime experiences and their gifts and talents, and their cultural background, the more you will understand about yourself and who you are'.

Have you ever spoken to your namer about your name? If they have died, is it possible to speak to a friend or a relative as Gary did? Are there records that may give clues as to the history of the family and/or the context in which the name-giver found themselves when you were given the name?

Tony Blair was seen as a hero in Kosovo due to the involvement of NATO in the conflict with Serbia. This then led to many young men born in or just after 1999 being given variations of his name. In an article from *The Guardian*, Julian Borger notes, 'It is not exactly a mass phenomenon, but it is the embodiment of one: a deep, national reverence for the man they consider their saviour'.[9] However, it's not just about a celebration of someone from the past; it's a name that has the desire to inspire the carrier of the name, and when Julian interviewed one young man, it seemed that the baton had been picked up: 'Fifteen years on, Tonibler Sahiti is doing well at school and likes fixing electronic gear in his spare time; he would like to design websites. "I feel very good when people call my name," he says. "I would like to achieve something like Prime Minister Blair did. To save people from wars."' Tonibler Sahiti was looking at the past, looking to the future and then determining how to live in the present.

Many people would point to aspects of Tony Blair's life that they feel would discount him from deserving such a profound legacy, but something has inspired Tonibler. Something has 'influenced or animated [Tonibler] with an idea or purpose'. It's far too easy for us to discount the significance of our forebears because of their failures or limitations but doing so has a cost. The cost is unproductivity. It's generation after generation having to redesign the wheel, rather than standing on the shoulders of those who have gone before.

This burden of propagating the baton has always intrigued me. I used to love watching the Olympic games when I was growing up, and was fascinated by the Greek origins and the superhuman feat of training for four years to compete in a single event. In the Atlanta games of 1996, gold medals were scarce for British Olympians. I remember the expectation building for the 4x100m relay race: Linford Christie, gold medal winner from the last Olympics, and the others looked so strong. However Great Britain didn't even qualify from the heats. The baton wasn't passed effectively. Watching the devastation on the faces of the athletes was heartbreaking.

The song 'One Weak Link' from the film *The Prince of Egypt* is incredibly powerful. It refers to the heavy burden of responsibility that must have lain on the shoulders of each Pharaoh. With a dynasty stretching back over several millennia, who would want to be the one who failed, with the catastrophic consequences of the kingdom falling, the loss of credibility and power? This must have been a huge strain on each successive father and son.

Nevertheless, people make mistakes. Marriages collapse. Poverty, illness, and injustice can all lead to a perceived family failure. Perhaps your father failed, maybe your mother, and you don't feel that they deserve the honour of your carrying their name forward. Perhaps you have failed, and you don't feel worthy to speak a destiny into being with any true conviction.

As mentioned earlier, in chapter six I share transcripts of interviews I conducted with people from diverse cultures. One of the key findings was the desire to honour earlier generations in the naming of the following generations. How and even whether these names would be recognised and celebrated varied. However, the fact remains that the way forward involved a significant contemplation of the road that had already been walked. Were you named after a parent, or a grandparent? Is there a family name that is being passed like a baton from generation to generation in your family, or does that not matter to you? It didn't matter to me when I was involved in the process of being a 'namer'. Despite all I have already told you, at the time, regrettably, I was captivated by a greater sense of looking forward than looking back. I do wonder why that was. How about you and your experiences? Maybe family breakdown plays a bigger part than first thought. Should you include the name of your mum, your stepmum, or the lady that your dad's now with, five years since your mum's death? Maybe you never met your father, your mum won't speak about him, or his name would just be too painful for her and other relatives.

Three examples of receiving a name

Not every namer has a 'rending of the heavens' experience, for example where a name is given in a dream. We have looked at different ways a name feels right, but the key is to find the heart in the naming. Sometimes it takes someone else to see it.

Let me share more of Rudi's story with you (which I mentioned at the beginning of this book), as well as the stories of two others who felt that the generation of their names were inauspicious.

Rudi's father grew up in Benevento in southern Italy. Tito was the quintessential Italian, a lover of his country, of family, food, fine wine, and above all, football. He loved Napoli – a team that he had supported since he was a child – and at the point of the birth of his son, a Dutch import by the name of Rudolf Jozef Krul was making a significant impression on supporters. Krul was a sublime left back/sweeper who had taken the Dutch captaincy from Cruyff and was heralded as a true coup for Napoli amongst the Italian league. Krul-mania apparently ensued. He was elegantly strong and quick on both sides. With majestic heading capabilities, a phenomenal long pass, and the personality to match all of these, Krul was the Rolls Royce of football – certainly in the eyes of the Neapolitans. Decades later when the current manager Maurizio Sarri met Krul, this greeting was unsurprising: 'Grande Rudy, you are a Napoli hero. You are Napoli!'[10] It's not surprising then that Tito bestowed this name on his son. By exploring this insight into Rudi's father, you come to know the father, what moves him, what gives him life. How wonderful for Rudi to be able to share this with his father, particularly while watching their favourite team. 'Forza Napoli!'

One friend I spoke to is from South Africa. She had also never explored her name, what it meant, or what was in the heart of the namer. However, after we had had a catch-up chat one day, she wrote to me about some sad news. Following our conversation, she had decided to get in touch with her mum and find out what was in her heart when the name was given. She sent me a text with what seemed to be a heavy heart. 'My oldest sister gave me my name,' she wrote. 'There was a girl in her class named Melanie, and Google says my name means blackness, dark. So, nothing interesting.' I replied to her that on the contrary, this spoke to me of the relationship between her mum and older sister, that her mum listened to and valued the input of a child. I pointed out how precious this heart attitude was and that it demonstrated a loving relationship. Melanie was taken aback: 'You're right, William, yes, they are so close; thank you'. With a small piece of investigation and asking the right questions, she had come to appreciate her name and her namer in a new and meaningful way.

The last example happened just this week. A young woman in her early twenties named Demi told me that her name wasn't very special: she was named after Demi Moore. I asked her if her namer had explained why. She told me that her mum and dad had watched the film *Ghost* early in their courtship and it had meant a lot to both of them, as individuals, but it became significant as a marker in their relationship. I thought for a moment then challenged her. 'This gives me a real insight into them. Your mum and dad were so moved by a film that talks about love that carries on after death that they wanted to give you this name. That the name of this actor stirred something in them of a joint experience that they wanted to remember when they said your name? I would say that that was significant.' Demi nodded her head thoughtfully, she told me that she was moved, she had never seen it like that before.

***

The heart behind this chapter was to give you the chance to consider reframing your understanding of your name in relation to two aspects that we all engage with: your identity as an individual and your identity as part of a community through the relationship with your namer. We each have a responsibility to ourselves as well as to those around us to know who we are. This is a key part of ensuring that we play our part in history well. Not that we seek to be lauded or celebrated unnecessarily, but that we can say that we have tried to be an effective link in a chain or carrier of a baton, to honour those before us and to give every opportunity for generations that follow to thrive as they stand on our shoulders.

This chapter has had a golden thread of reconciliation running through it. Do you remember how we defined reconciliation as 'to restore to union and friendship after estrangement or variance'? As I encourage you to seek out the heart of your namer, the call is to reconciliation.

History clearly proves that diverse cultures and civilisations at different times have been good and bad at this, so in the following chapter we will explore how names and naming are dealt with in various cultures around the world and consider what wisdom can be gleaned from them.

6

To Receive Another

If you are going to be an heiress, you can't have a normal name, unless you're British. All British people have plain names, and that works pretty well over there. But in America, you've got to have a name that stands out.

Paris Hilton[1]

How do various cultures view names and the process of naming?

This chapter explores naming as a global phenomenon; that irrespective of tribe, value system, quality of life or perceived engagement with modernity, culture associated with naming is, and has always been, significant. My hope is that through reading and considering these interviews you will be enriched in your understanding, and that an appetite for seeking to connect with people through their names will have been whetted.

***

An explosion of xenophobic sentiment ripped apart lives, families and communities in South Africa in 2008. Those from local tribes who shared part of the national identity were becoming increasingly intolerant of immigrants from Somalia, Mozambique and Zimbabwe whom they saw as setting up competitive businesses and taking their jobs. I remember one teenager who came to me distraught, his family having died as their home had been torched while he was out playing football. My volunteer work with the church took on a new focus as we sought out and administrated resources that came flooding in, from mountains of food to warehouses for homeless families. We counselled and supported young leaders from all parts of the affected communities. This battle of and over identity absolutely arrested me and became fundamentally formative. The ancient Greek word *xenos* is key to understanding xenophobia. It was the word used to describe something that was strange, foreign, alien, something other. The fear of something strange has repeatedly led to horrors throughout history, and this chapter will, I trust, encourage you to desire to learn from, rather than fear, an other. The key to this chapter is that a name is a window to a culture. It's an invitation to something beyond our understanding. The word *culture* is defined as 'the way of life, especially the general customs and beliefs, of a particular group of people at a particular time',[2] but to really get a deeper sense of the word, please meditate on its root. Etymologically, culture is to do with the Latin word *cultura*, which is 'the tilling of land, act of preparing the earth for crops'.[3] I'd like to propose that the culture of a society is the environment in which a life receives the seeds that will be sown into it, to ensure that the seeds are given the best opportunity to thrive so that they will in themselves produce more seeds. By studying other cultures, we are forced to consider why a certain people group would make the effort to prepare the soil of a life in a certain way, what value they see in the seeds, and the long-term view of generations of seed-bearing plants.

'Do yourself a favour and get some hiking boots.'

How open are you to consider the wisdom of others? I often don't, then suffer the consequences. I'd decided to do an 'Xtreme Character Challenge' to connect with a bunch of guys who go off into the wild for days at a time, hiking up mountains, camping, and talking about stuff that many of us rarely talk about. I was pretty fit but still recognised the need to put in some training beforehand. Twice a week I'd take my rucksack stuffed with weights and towels to simulate the pack I'd have to carry, put my trainers on and set off for yo-yo manoeuvres up my local hill. A few of the guys I was going to go with had arranged to do a practice hike up a Welsh mountain three weeks beforehand, and I arrived with my rucksack feeling a real nervous excitement. One of the guys came up to me and said with palpable confusion, 'Where are your hiking boots?' 'It's fine,' I replied, 'these are great trainers,' as I showed him the grip underneath. 'OK mate…' came the reply.

I'm still reluctant to say categorically that I wouldn't have rolled my ankle if I'd been wearing proper hiking boots, but in retrospect my pride got in the way. How was I to know that Brian had done Mt Kilimanjaro twenty-four times (yes, he's the one who climbs unclimbed peaks from chapter three) and actually knew what he was talking about? I had taken my understanding and my experience and decided that that was all I needed. We don't know it all; every sip we take from another's cup enlightens us. This chapter will allow you to taste other cultures' perspectives on naming.

Encounters with a different culture can prove challenging when the culture is far removed from our way of life. For me, French, Spanish and Italian names are easy: similar alphabet, similar sounds, similar lifestyle. German, Swedish, Greek and Ukrainian are a step away, but names with clicks like Xhosa, or written from right to left or using very different alphabets have me struggling. Take a moment to imagine this caricature of a brolly-brandishing English gentleman: He hesitates on meeting someone from outside his cultural bubble. 'Sorry old chap, what was your name again? Jolly good… and how would one spell that? [Long pause] Right… do you mind if I call you… Tim?' It's laughable to imagine being this ignorant to ask, or gracious enough to comply, but sadly, as you will read shortly, it still happens. Most of us try to get names right, but the temptation to either avoid this cultural clash or somehow negate it is desperately sad. Try to empathise with the pain Dennis Quaid experienced while presenting the 2015 Golden Globes. Gripping the podium tightly with both hands, Dennis read the list of nominations for Best Actress in a Drama. The world watched the confident, cocky charisma with which he proffered the first two nominations noticeably erode as he announced the third, then vanish as he stumbled over the name of the fourth nominee: 'Sheesha' Ronan. He had clearly been concerned about mispronouncing it and rightly so, for he had botched it. How did Saoirse respond? With grace. We can never know how she felt on the inside, but the subject was broached during an interview on the TV show *This Morning* where she was asked how she felt when people couldn't pronounce her name. She talked about how it had annoyed her as a child but that she has become more gracious over time, even finding it humorous now.

Would you fear getting it wrong and so try to force the other into your paradigm? In my experience, the joy and appreciation shown by the other at my efforts to get a name right is utterly compelling. I often come across individuals who introduce themselves to me as one thing, then say, 'but feel free to call me…. [insert anglicised/more readily accessible version here] instead'. This chapter can be your starter pack, a baptism through names into worlds different to yours that offer up insight into culture, mindsets and tradition – and which may prompt you to consider your own.

***

Wee Kek Koon, a translator and former columnist for the *South China Morning Post*, thanked me as I offered him the forum to share his experience.

> 'My name is the only link I have with her [his grandmother who named him]. For me personally, I treasure this name; it's a form of respect to retain this name. This is why I have not taken on an English name, which is very popular among Chinese communities around the world. And thank you very much by the way for calling me by that name "Kek Koon". You've been to Hong Kong, so you know people take on English names, whether that's Peter, Paul or Mary, but I've not done that.'

'Kek Koon' means 'to overcome many obstacles', a meaning which this man deeply holds to and values. Why would he choose to forsake the honour the name holds for his ancestor, or the significance of what it means for him in his journey through life? Or rather, why should he?

The question is, as we become more 'modern' and perceive ourselves to be increasingly 'advanced', are we losing this sense of honour and respect that is a foundation of intergenerational connectivity and ultimately society itself? How is it that reverence for the heart behind the name leads to a depth of communication that opens doors, while a negative, disrespectful response from the hearer can lead to alienation and a sense of loss?

The Iranian-American human rights activist Mahnaz Afkhami wrote this: 'We have the ability to achieve, if we master the necessary goodwill, a common global society blessed with a shared culture of peace that is nourished by the ethnic, national and local diversities that enrich our lives'.[4] This chapter will aid you in raising your awareness of the intricacies, honour and beauty of others' naming practices and names themselves. My heart is that we all become eager hearers, that on an introduction we treasure the name shared as something of value, that as we hear it, we feel curious to know its purpose, the heart of the culture behind it and ultimately something of the identity of the individual who carries it.

The meat of this chapter is drawn from interviews I conducted with individuals from China, Iceland, Iran, Japan, Mongolia, Singapore and Zimbabwe – the tip of a globally intercultural iceberg that I vow to continue to be enlightened by. I will share their stories; stories of how they were named, the ways their culture has affected how they hold their name, the desire for this to be understood and accepted by others and often how this has influenced their choices as namers.

***

The first section of text is from a conversation I had with a friend of mine called Rachel. Rachel is from China and was introduced to me by a mutual friend who is heavily involved with the Liverpool China Partnership:

> 'My Chinese name is Yang Luenn. The family name – in my case, Yang – goes first. My given name, Luenn, was given to me by my father because I was born on Middle Autumn Day, which is a full moon festival in China. Luenn means circle and relates to the full moon, and "round" in Chinese also means happiness. This is what my father wanted me to be: happy and surrounded by family. As you might imagine, names are an expectation for our life and future. My brother's first name is Dragon because he was born during the year of the dragon – thus the expectation that he would have a bright future and be very powerful. His trajectory didn't go in this direction, however, and my father changed my brother's name before his eighteenth birthday because he was a troublemaker and had been the cause of many complaints from school and other peers.
>
> The Chinese believe that the universe is made from five elements that need to operate in balance: metal, wood, fire, water and air. As is a common practice in China, my father went to a fortune teller who told him that my brother lacked metal and water elements. He suggested that my father change my brother's name to help balance these two elements and see him come back to the right track. After this, my brother did cause less trouble, but maybe this was because he grew older and matured, I don't know!
>
> When a newborn baby turns 100 days old, we have a celebration where we lay out several things for a baby to choose: a dictionary, a pen, money, or other things

that represent money, knowledge, or power. Parents use these to see which the baby chooses and believe that this is what the kid will chase through life – knowledge or money or power. I don't really believe in these things; however, my friends did this last year for their baby boy. They put five or ten things on the floor and noticed that the first thing the baby grabbed was a dictionary. So, they said, "This boy is going to be very good at studies; he may achieve a very high level of education in the future."

My husband and I named our daughter Zehan. Ze means "daughter" and Han means "kind, self-disciplined or well-behaved". We wish her to be a person who is nice and kind and self-disciplined, and actually, she is! It's interesting, I had never thought about the relationship between her name and its possible impact before.'

I was struck by the unquestioning connection Rachel made between an individual's name and their nature. I also found the 100 days custom wonderful, in that it showed a belief that the child has an innate desire or vision for its life, a desire that it is unconsciously aware of from an early age, and that by, in a sense, revealing this to the parents, they will be able to more effectively partner with the child in preparing them to attain their vision or their deepest desires.

***

The following text is taken from a conversation I had with an Icelandic designer friend of mine, Sigrún. I worked with Sigrún during a project in Camden where I was stimulated by how she incorporated Icelandic images, materials and cultural references in her clothing designs:

'In Icelandic traditions, names all mean something. We are very similar to the Native Americans in that names are descriptive. They can be personifications, but they are usually descriptive of something tangible, emotional, or often mythological. Also, we don't have surnames or family names; we have given names and reference names. My name is Sigrún Björk, but my reference name is Ólafsdóttir which means that I'm the daughter of Ólafur. My brother is Ólafsson, son of Ólafur. My mother is Hlöðversdóttir, and my father is Tryggvason, because Tryggvi was the name of his father. It's very genealogical and this is why a wife doesn't take her husband's name.

If you read the Icelandic Sagas, every book starts by explaining the genealogical connection of a person. So, a book would start like this: "Sigrún Björk who lived in this town, daughter of Ólafur, son of Tryggvi, son of Gísli", and it would go back generations. Genealogy is a huge thing in Iceland. The government has a database where every Icelander has been mapped, since the beginning of time they have been studying it and writing it down. It used to be like this in all the Nordic countries, but Norway, Denmark and Sweden don't do this anymore. Take your name – Thompson. That's an old Nordic way of naming, so you will definitely have had a Nordic ancestor that has been handed down in your name.

When I had my two boys, we named the first one after his paternal grandfather and my younger son is Ólafur. If in the future he was to have a daughter and named her Sigrún Björk after me, she would have exactly the same name as me, so it's almost a chain and a culture of honour generation after generation. You can see this in the history books, sometimes for 20 generations with two male names, each after each other, which becomes well known – a family brand almost.'

I was so taken by the importance Sigrún placed on naming that I explored a second part of our conversation in the following chapter where we study name changing. Her determination to hold onto naming traditions inspired me and the research it prompted led me to uncover a fascinating link between naming, language and culture.

**

I became friends with Hilal, the source of our next cultural insight, because of my son. He became close friends with Ali at primary school and his father and I would often talk at length as the boys played. I was always blessed by his hospitality and openness:

> 'I am Hilal Hussein Al Libawe. Al Libawe is not my surname, it's my extended family name. We call it here "El Hasheera" which is a group name or a community. There are 10,000 or more here in Babylon called "Al Libawe" while some family groups in Iraq can number around a million. My father is Abdul Hussein. Hilal means "crescent". When the moon starts after the New Moon, it's Hilal. This is how we date our Arabic months and major calendar events such as Ramadan, Eid and the Hajj.
>
> My son is Ali, which is a famous name in Islam because it's the son-in-law of Mohammed through Mohammed's daughter Fatima. It means a "high thing", a rising up. My brother is called Ali, his son is called Ali, my cousin is Ali; we have many people called Ali in our family! Names are significant because you didn't choose your name, it was your father or your parents who chose it, and I agree with you that this affects the personality. Usually when you say

> Ali you think of something great. Of course, there are exceptions though. Usually, we don't change our names from birth to death; it's a very complicated process as it's significant for a person to carry this name throughout his or her life.'

I was particularly drawn to what Hilal said about the practice of naming as a response to the awareness of celestial markers, phases of the moon, stars etc., and how they are also reflected in Hindu naming practices. They rely on Vedic astrology to arrive at the name of a child and there is a wonderfully elaborate process that culminates in the Namkaran ritual. I also found it fascinating that his name connected him to a wider group or community. I considered how this would be of significance were an individual to lose their immediate family, but also the importance of community relationships, something rarely tapped into in Western traditions.

***

Next, we hear from Masumi who is from Japan but is based in London. She was introduced to me by my brother:

> 'My name Masumi was given to me by my godfather who was also a gynaecologist and helped my mum deliver me. Masumi means "truly pure" or "truly honest". As we choose a name, we consider how the kanji characters best fit together and will often get advice from a monk or anyone who is an expert on strokes as even the number of character strokes is important for future good luck. I think this possibly comes from a Chinese influence, that the strokes matter, because some numbers are not very nice. The number 4 is し (shi) and the number 9 is く (ku) and these sound the same as the words for death (死, shi) and agony (苦, ku). Because of this we don't want to

use that sound and we don't want to use that number of strokes.

Japanese names are very interesting in this way. They aren't just about sound but about the characters that compose them. Two people can have the same sounding name but if they're written with different characters, there would be different meanings. We usually use more ordinary characters, but there are also ancient kanji characters that are not easy to read straight away. It's a bit more complicated than writing in an alphabet I suppose!

In the Buddhist tradition, a new name is given to a person at the temple after their death. This is called a kymeo; it's when you become a part of Buddha. A few weeks later, the monks will give the kymeo to the relatives engraved on a decorative stick and this is what will also be engraved on the gravestone. It's very traditional and people sometimes worry about it; it's become a bit of a business. These days, many will purchase the name from the monk before the person has even died. Traditionally this kymeo was all about how long a person had lived or how high ranking they were from having served the temple, but I was reading a while ago about how money is influencing this ritual nowadays. One enterprising company decided to give people a "better deal" at a particular price, but then the Japanese Buddhist Association put a stop to this.

I'm married to an English man, Matthew, and when we thought about naming our children, we wanted the names to be unique and connected to both our cultures and also carry a significant meaning. We decided to call our daughter Maria, but with a slightly

> different pronunciation and with Japanese characters (真璃杏). The first character "Ma" is the same as mine, the second is "Ri" which means sparkle or glassy, and the last part "A" is a character for apricot. A fruit-associated name is also a little wish for Maria's life, that it would be filled with her success, not only financially but as a life.
>
> Our son Leo's name went through a similar process. Leo is pronounced more like "Lio" here in the UK, but in Japan we don't have the "Li" sound, so it will be "Ri" instead of "Li" in his Japanese passport. The Japanese characters he has are 璃音, Ri (Li) has the same sound and character as his sister (sparkle, glassy) and the second character "O" connotes music or sound.'

I was amazed at the various levels of engagement with a name that Masumi shared about, that even the number of strokes in the written version of the name mattered. I also found it interesting that the conferring of a new name could be exploited. What a fascinating balance – that the more mysterious the process behind naming is, the more vulnerable you would be to the gatekeepers of the mystery.

***

Rina is from Mongolia and is based in Liverpool. We were brought together by a mutual friend and share a love for culture, language and rowing:

> 'My name is Mongolian, but it's taken on various iterations at Chinese school, in Japan, and now here in the UK upon getting married and taking my husband's surname. Getting married in the UK and changing my surname was not difficult at all. I felt different as soon as people started calling me Rina Sowler, even

though I am obviously physically and biologically still the same being. It has given me a different social status and I was suddenly an English Chinese Mongolian; it was bizarre. My Chinese surname did not give me much instant recognition; I gained recognition myself by working hard and studying hard to make my name known at the University in Japan. My English name, however, has given me instant recognition from close social groups and business associations as it bears a much stronger and well-known family name. I appreciate the benefits of being a Sowler as a member of a loving family. I do miss, however, being Rina Wu (吴日娜), when people saw me and me only.

Will your name change the path of your life? Will your name decide where you go from a certain point? Women in China do not change their maiden names after getting married. Does that mean they are more themselves than women married in the UK who willingly or unwilling bear their husbands' names? I'm not sure. As you said in your [YouTube] video, is it your name that defines you or do you grow into some sort of identity that defines your name? It really is such an intriguing question.

My parents are Mongolian. For political reasons, my parents had to adapt my name to a Chinese version for me to be able to go to school and be able to work. You can't just have a Mongolian name; you have to have a Chinese name. So, my Chinese name is 吴日娜, where 吴 is my surname, Wu. In China I'm 日 (rì) 娜 (nà) but in Mongolian the pronunciation would be "wulurna" and written differently. This is a very popular Mongolian girl's name; it's like Mary. My Father was very academic, and he wanted me to stand out as such, so he changed the first character, "cloud" 乌 (wū), to "mouth above the sky" 吴 (wú) (as 乌 and 吴 are homophones).

In China, naming a boy is completely different to naming a girl. "Shame naming" at birth is a long-standing tradition for baby boys. The birth of a baby boy would be greatly celebrated as the heir and future. But funnily enough, the family would give the boy a very ugly, insignificant, almost insulting name as a baby. For example, they would call the boy "Little dog 狗子" or "Dog's tail 狗尾巴" because according to Chinese superstition, if you gave the boy a very loud and grand name, the gods above would notice – "Oh, there's a boy, he's good, I want him" – and the parents would fear that a certain god above would take their boy away from them before his time. When the boy grew into a healthy child of four or five years old and the family believed that the boy could continue to grow older and healthier as he was going into school, they would give him a proper name that would go with him for the rest of his life to promote and advance his identity and strengthen the family tree.

Traditionally, a first-born girl would be named "Chow Dee" (招弟), Chow (招) meaning "to invite" and Dee (弟) meaning "little brother". Yes! There were a lot of "Chow Dees" in Chinese villages. The girl's purpose was to help the family pray for a male heir.

A racially, religiously and nationality-mixed family like mine will always have an intriguing story to tell regarding naming. For our first daughter, my mum got involved to make sure her name carried my Chinese Mongolian identity. My mother gave her a Mongolian name as her middle name, which sounds very much like "Angela". There are some well-known wild geese living on Mongolian grassland that migrate every year, and my mum very much hopes that Ivy will travel/migrate between the UK and China when she is older. We also wanted to celebrate her Englishness and commemorate her great-grandmother. Hence, we have Ivy Angela Sowler.

My second daughter is named Eva and she named herself: On the night before the baby scan, I dreamt of her and she was speaking in Mandarin, saying to me, "My name is Eva – E V A – this is how you spell it." I woke up and thought, "OK!" Her middle name is to honour Grandma from the English side of the family.

Talking about their names has helped me realise how we as namers are trying to create our children's identities for them and hope they could carry the meanings with them and define themselves both as Sowlers and as Wus.'

I was taken by Rina's journey in reconciling two such distinct worlds, honouring her Mongolian heritage as well as the culture she has married into. This dance of honour and respect is a story that is reflected in and accessed through her name and the names of her children.

***

As I mentioned earlier, I reached out to Kek Koon after reading a compelling article he had written in the *South China Morning Post* on demystifying Chinese names. This is an extract from one of our conversations:

'I'm Chinese Singaporean, born in Singapore. I moved to Hong Kong 20 years ago and now I'm in Kuala Lumpur. Primarily I'm a translator of Chinese texts.

The first thing we need to explore is romanisation. Obviously, Chinese names are written in Chinese characters. So, for example, my name "Wee Kek Koon" is actually the romanisation of the characters 黃克群. It's an approximation of the pronunciation as it is in the original tongue; these romanisation systems vary over different regions. My name is based on the pronunciation in the Hokkien dialect, which is a Southern Chinese dialect. By the spelling of my name, and the way it is romanised people can see where I am from.

The family name (surname) is always put in front, which is why I don't like the terms "first name" and "last name" because this is, for want of a better term, Eurocentric, whereas for East Asians (not just Chinese – Koreans, Vietnamese, Japanese), our surnames are always put in front. In Malaysia, the Malays have no surname, and so in my passport there is no separate column for "surname" and "given name", it's just "name"! I think it's so important that people know that there are other naming conventions rather than just first name/last name as some sort of standard.

Kek Koon (克群) means "to overcome multiple obstacles". I was actually given my name by my paternal grandmother. She was quite a learned lady for her time, and she was a schoolteacher. She passed away in her early 50s and I never met her. My name is the only link I have with her. This is why I have not taken on an English name, a very popular practice among Chinese communities around the world. And thank you very much by the way for calling me by that name Kek Koon. You've been to Hong Kong, so you know people take on English names, whether that's Peter, Paul or Mary, but I've not done that.

In my culture, it's not good to have the same name as members of the older generations within the same family. So, my name should not be the same, or share the same characters, as my uncles or my grandfather's brothers. We tend not to use the same characters across generations; the name can have the same meaning, but we just use different characters. This is out of respect. There is also traditionally a name taboo (though not as common in modern times). Children are not allowed to, or supposed to, articulate their parent's name out loud. This is left over from a time when names were almost considered sacred, when you just wouldn't speak your parents' names and you wouldn't even speak other people's names. They would instead go by a nickname or scholarly name.

The nickname thing is really very interesting, because in Hong Kong, and increasingly in parts of Southeast Asia, this nickname is becoming synonymous with English names. So, for example, I know a person called Michael in Hong Kong. Michael Wong. He is known throughout his entire career, maybe even his life, as Michael. I may not ever come to know his real name unless he chooses to tell me.'

I find it incredible that in so many cultures there is such a deep desire to honour previous generations. However, the way to do that can be demonstrably opposite. In this culture the honour comes from not having the same name, or even verbalising it. However, in Iceland the honour comes from repeating it, seeing it recognised and acknowledged, and similarly in Africa there is a culture of honour in using the names of ancestors. Kek Koon's insight into naming taboos reminded me of ancient Egyptian naming practices and the concept of 'Ren' which we will go into in more detail in later chapters. Here also a child lived his life with a different name to avoid anyone learning his real one.

***

The individual I interviewed from Zimbabwe asked to remain anonymous, but she is a good friend of mine who works in health and is honoured and loved amongst the global community of Liverpool. Her insight and wisdom are well-recognised in Zimbabwe itself:

> 'There are differences in traditional practices amongst tribes, as well as between different areas of Zimbabwe. Usually, city dwellers and the younger generation don't seem to hold onto traditional practices fiercely, being away from rural homes and villages.
>
> Traditionally in Shona culture, the baby's name automatically goes to the father's line. The father has the dominance as the mother has left her family and joined his. If he is modern, then he can take her perspective to his family; however, his family may have already chosen a name. After a family discussion, if the child is to be named after a dead relative, then there is a significant aspect to the ceremony. If I can put it in English terms, it is similar to Asian views: a reincarnation of that mother or that grandmother in that daughter, or uncle to son, etc. There can be chanting, and the name is invoked, that spirit is believed to have transferred to the child, and that person grows up with that belief, that they are carrying their grandmother. As they grow up people will notice

things – "Oh, the grandmother used to do that!" So, when people are born, it's sometimes viewed as not of their own doing; it is their parents trying to honour their ancestors, and if you don't tend to do that, they will say that the family tends to suffer bad luck. So, in order to appease the late ones, they will continue with that name.

These are their African names. Because they go to school and experience the influence of the Western world – and in the past the impact of apartheid, where people didn't bother to pronounce, let alone understand these African names – nicknames like "Tuppence", "Big head boy" or "Jonny" would be given. Bad, silly, derogatory names. This was the influence of whites, that they felt that they had the right because they were white, that they had power over these guys. Because of this, most people have an English name now, so at school maybe he is known as Christopher, but at home in his village, he is known as Rugaray.

Sometimes the name relates more to the situation surrounding the birth of the child. If the man has rejected the wife or cast her out and she has gone, pregnant, she will call the child "Rejection" or "You left me" or "Never again" or "Never". Or "Love more", because the man wasn't liking her too much, or he denied her, and by calling the child this he would love her more. Or she's the second or third wife and she wants more of that love, because she's coming from a tribe or a marriage where they practice polygamy. Or the child is called "Jealous" for a similar reason. There was a man who was called "Nobody" because the father had rejected him. He refused to have anything to do with this child. So, the woman said "Ah, you are leaving me as a nobody", so her situation dictated that this was his name. After years being in a Christian environment where he was constantly encouraged to believe that he was a somebody, he decided to change his name. You're not going to guess what it was that he changed his name to! Honestly… he changed his name to "Somebody"!'

I enjoyed how her insights stimulate the nature/nurture debate and to what extent the naming is complicit when an individual starts to behave in a way that echoes the individual they were named after. Her case studies of individuals who have been named out of pain galvanised a thread of thought I continue in the last chapter of this book.

***

One of the consistent themes that came across during these interviews was the sense that the traditional ways are being lost. Often it was said in this way: 'This is what happened traditionally, but now it only really happens in the villages'. Or, 'As members of this modern generation, we do things differently'. This leads me to wonder whether in our modern world we are becoming so much wiser or whether, ironically, we are losing wisdom. The Bible puts it like this, 'Therefore every scribe who has become a disciple of the kingdom of heaven is like a head of a household, who brings out of his treasure new things and old' (Matthew 13:52 NASB). Do we embrace this balance, taking what was good from the past and also reaching into the new?

In the same way that we face the danger of losing our cultural heritage, many are losing the heritage of intergenerational relationships, for all sorts of reasons. One of the results of this, I believe, is that names are losing their significance, honour and respect, just as the namers are. And if something loses its value, it can easily be tossed away.

***

I would like to encourage you to make a personal commitment in response to this chapter: to be intentionally inquisitive about names, and to demonstrate being interested in the individual standing before you. On a practical note, it will help you to remember the name, but exposing yourself to a culture through a name is like dipping your toe into another language and another world. And as Czech President, philosopher and hero Tomáš Garrigue Masaryk said at the end of the 19th century, 'Kolik jazyků znáš, tolikrát jsi člověkem',[5] which translates as 'The more languages you know, the more human you are'. In almost every interaction I experience with someone from another culture I find that showing an interest in their full name is received with an excited gratitude, as they see that I am aware of the significance of the given name, particularly as it reflects an interest in family and culture beyond the individual. It's this interest that develops openness and trust and ultimately helps to build bridges between individuals and communities.

Introduction to Part Three

Would you remember names if they meant more to you? I was watching a video by Thomas Frank on why people forget names. He said that it's because names are so arbitrary. He actually called them 'arbitrary strings of letters and syllables that don't mean a whole lot'.[1] If something is arbitrary, the dictionary tells us that it is 'based on whim or personal preference, without reason or pattern; random'.[2] This could be why it's so hard to file names well, and why it's crucial to find something more to them… to give them life.

I had no idea how many Volvo SUVs there were on the road, but as soon as I started looking at buying one, I saw them everywhere. I remember this happening when I oversaw the suit department at River Island as a young man, I suddenly started noticing the suits people were wearing and whether they fitted them or not. When you are aware of something, you notice it, when you look for something, you see it. This is known as the Baader-Meinhof phenomenon. Ann Pietrangelo wrote about it in 2019: 'In short, Baader-Meinhof phenomenon is a frequency bias. You notice something new, at least it's new to you. It could be a word, a breed of dog, a particular style of house, or just about anything. Suddenly, you're aware of that thing all over the place. In reality, there's no increase in occurrence. It's just that you've started to notice it'.[3] The key is the final sentence – 'It's just that you've started to notice it'. This phenomenon is not the answer, it's not that we weren't aware of names, it's just that we have the capacity to notice them more. The key takes us back to the intentionality I spoke about in the introduction. A name is only arbitrary if you see no life in it, but when you do… seeing that it matters helps it find its way into long-term memory. When you see something truly for what it is, you give it life. This is what happens when we inspire people, we breathe life into them.

I'd go further and say that the purpose of these next three chapters is to help you *recognise* names. To recognise means more than you may realise. The 'cognise' part is to do with knowing; the 're' part is to do with going back to or changing something. So when you recognise, you change the way you think about something. I'm convinced that as we explore the mystery of names and naming it will jog your memory and you will realise that actually you knew these things all along.

Part three is a further exploration into the mystery of names and naming.

To change a name – if you believe that your name is arbitrary then you will find it easier to change.

To give a name – when you recognise that names are significant, the weight of the decision over them is greater. You see the value in taking the decision over a name with more care.

To be a name – what is the ultimate mystery behind a name.

Interviews

I have included two interviews below that will help to orientate your thinking as we step into chapter seven.

The first is screen- and theatre-trained actor and general fitness fanatic Carmen, an individual I connected with during my research who is based in London and has Asian roots.

The second is with singer/songwriter M, who I also connected with during my research. Also based in London and hailing from European and North African roots, she asked to be referred to as 'M' instead of her full name. The interview was conducted while M was nonbinary, however she is now a transgender woman.

Carmen

'My parents are from Hong Kong, but I was born in London, so I have Chinese heritage but feel quite disconnected from my Chinese side. It was my parents who named me, and mostly my father. My Western name is Carmen and taken after a character from one of my favourite films when I was a teenager: Starship Troopers. It wasn't because it had meaning for me, I just liked the sound of it. I guess I wanted something unusual for myself rather than something ordinary. My mom said that she had wanted to give me a different Western name after the midwife, but I said no. I've never met the midwife; maybe if I'd met her, it would have had been significant for me, more interesting.

As I was growing up, I used my Chinese name until I was in my teens and then I switched to my Western name. All the way through school — and this sounds really mean — whenever people called me by my Chinese name, I didn't like it. It took me a while to realise why I didn't like it: people pronounced it wrong. Growing up in a very white area where people were very racist, they didn't really care about my name. They made a joke out of it, particularly what it rhymed with. The other reason was that when people whined at me, they elongated my name. It just sounded horrible, and I didn't like it.

When I got to my teens I decided to change to my Western name. On paper my name was still officially my Chinese name, but at college, university, then work, I always asked people to call me Carmen. It started getting really complicated, because they had to remember both names. I remember during A levels, there was one teacher who rolled her eyes when I told her what I like to be called when she was taking the register. I just remember the look in her eyes, as if saying, "Oh, another person who wants to be westernised." She wasn't very nice to me; she just made me feel horrible. That stuck with me, and I really felt like those who didn't know me didn't deserve to call me by my Chinese name. Because I liked my Western name, I decided that that's all I was going to give people.

As far as my surname is concerned, in all cultures your surname is very important to you because it carries your father's name, your father's genes or history or whatever. But my father became estranged from me during my teens, and when that happened, I thought, "That's it. He doesn't deserve anything from me. I'm going to change my surname. I'm not going to be known by his surname. I'm going to have my own surname and start my own legacy."

At the time, I felt really pleased. I felt more independent. I felt that this was serious; I wasn't doing it to have fun, I actually meant it. I also felt that this was going to make life so much easier, particularly for the people that I worked with. I was being logical and practical to save a lot of headaches. But also, I was so angry when my father became estranged from me. I'd been trying for years to build a relationship with him, but he changed his phone number as if he'd forgotten that I existed. As that was the only way that I could contact him, I felt that that was a sign of complete disregard for me. Thus, it felt natural to disregard his surname since he'd disregarded me. I didn't want anything that he'd given me any more. It wasn't an easy decision but at the time it felt like the right thing to do.

What if my dad had found out that I changed his name? There wasn't any point in taking into consideration his feelings any more, or anyone else's, in regard to my name change. It was my decision. Besides, the surname that I made for myself wasn't a name that I plucked out of nowhere. It was an amalgamation of my Chinese surname and something else. So, I didn't completely lose my father's surname, I simply took his surname and added other letters that meant something to me. It still has something of my father in it. And I want to carry that on to my children.

Two or three years ago my father passed away quite suddenly and everything I tried to get away from came back to me. It's taken a long period of time to forgive him. It was only a couple of months ago that I started thinking, "Was it the right thing to do to change the name?" Now that I've tried really hard to forgive him and I've tried to become more connected to my Chinese heritage, and to my concept of myself, I think maybe my Chinese name is very special.'

M

'I think it's really interesting for us to have this conversation. I am mixed race. My dad is Tunisian, and my mum is German, so M reflects my dad and Nicolas reflects my mom. My mum came up with Nicolas while watching a television programme, she heard the name Nichola and thought it was a very international name because there's Nicholas in English and Nicolas in German. My dad's brother had passed away before my birthday while my mother was pregnant, and it's traditional within North African communities, particularly Tunisia and Morocco, that the next born receives the name of the most recently deceased. My mum wasn't a big fan of the name, but she didn't have a choice. So, it's a compromise that they both chose a name. Since childhood my dad has always called me M. I personally preferred Nicolas as I was growing up, and I loved it when people called me Nikki. Then when I got into my early teens, I felt that Nikki was too much like a girl's name. I was having a kind of gender identity crisis and felt like I wanted to sound more like a boy. So, I think, because I was internally struggling with my gender identity, I wanted to portray myself as more masculine on the outside. So, I switched to Nick, and was known as Nick from when I was 13 until I was 17 or 18. [M refers to Nicolas as her deadname.]

I do a lot of music and started to use M as my stage name. For a very long time I felt I was alienated from my North African Arab identity because I don't fit any of the Arabic stereotypes. But as soon as I got out of those really moody teens I started wanting to reconnect with that culture and I started liking that name and using it all the time. When I moved to the UK, I realised that a lot of people in the UK didn't know what gender M was as a name. I just really liked that, that my name didn't necessarily represent a gender (even though it does in Arabic). So, I started using M more and more as it reflected my nonbinary identity which became more externally available to me, and I started expressing it in that way. I think a lot of nonbinary, or gender nonconforming people, refer to monosyllabic names or things that represent nature, but at the moment that still feels a bit alien to me. I'm having a really hard time right now because I know the true meaning of M. I know it's a very male name and does that really matter? Does an Arabic social perception of a name define my gender? I feel like I'd like to legally change it to something completely different. Or maybe I'll just stick with M for now and see how it feels. It's sort of dependent on how strong that inner perception of yourself is, because honestly, I do believe that names are just social communicators. I believe that my name doesn't define me, that there is just so much more in terms of my cultural lineage that manifests internally, whether it's my gender code, my facial features, or my skin tone. I think so much more defines me than my name. But it's more. Is it enough to have that sense of self identity, or do I somehow need to convey that to a society that isn't aware of all of that and will gender you or perceive you on superficial things like a name on a document or your external expression? So, it's a hard conversation and it's very dependent on an environment and how much that matters to someone else, actually.

I don't think that changing my name changes anything about my heritage, a name can easily be taken away from you; it can easily be changed. Just because you don't have access to knowledge of my personal heritage, because you can't read it in my face, or in my name any more, doesn't mean that it doesn't exist. This conversation is fascinating. It's making me think about things and question myself. It's making me think, "Would changing my name cut me off from my mum and my dad, or would I not be Tunisian any more?" No, no way. I'm as much Tunisian, and as much my mother's child as I am my father's child.

It's important to have your own sense of identity. Right now, I have no idea what I would change my name to, in all honesty. That's the difficulty I see, just because there is nothing that I feel would represent me right now, or that would allow me access to myself right now. If I was to reference the name, it would be personal experience and might be something I really like. River, for example, is a gender-neutral name. Or it might be this person I really look up to. But I think in that sense I might be performing something I admire or would aspire to be because you take on what you aspire to be. That then comes back to the question of, "Is that wrong at all?" because we're all just echoes of past experience or admiration towards certain things. Just as Nicolas, for example, is an admiration that my mom had towards a name that she heard. Does it change if I have admiration for a singer or something and I apply that to myself? So right now, I'm too early in the process to be able to have some sort of definitive name or reference point that I'd like to call myself. I just think that M is fitting for now, but I don't think that it's eternal in that sense. I'll just see how long it carries me because I feel like the name deserves me and I deserve the name, and I'm honouring it and honouring my dad's brother, my uncle. There's a mutual relationship that we share but I do think I see an expiry date on it. It really depends on how my identity evolves and what social circles I end up in, where it really doesn't matter anymore. There are so many other levels with career or relationships that could be an influence; it might be related to my health or my wealth. I might not even depend on something as trivial as my name or I might completely disassociate and feel that this really does matter and I need to see some kind of reflection of myself in a name because I don't see myself anywhere in life. I think it's something that's just going to crystallise in the next few years.

I think that thinking about these things and considering these things is so important, these questions have been here almost as long as humankind in that sense, and I think it's really important that you're exploring this … that you're looking for answers from so many different people and exploring all kinds of naming processes. That will give people the opportunity to evaluate and explore other people's experiences and then come to their own original conclusion. It's definitely very interesting and important to have this in literature to stir this conversation.'

7

To Change a Name

When I changed names, I put periods on those eras.
                                        Sean Love Combs[1]

How comfortable would you be in changing your name, and what would necessitate it? Perhaps a change in location, beliefs, gender or relationship with your namer. However, if an unwanted scarf is hard to return out of concerns about the feelings of the giver, how much harder the changing of a name!

The key thread of this book is reconciliation, and that through your name you connect with others, intergenerationally and otherwise, so it would follow that changing one's name could indicate that an irrevocable breakdown in relationships has taken place, or needs to take place. There are, of course, as many reasons to change a name as there are those who change them, so my hope is that this chapter will stimulate clarity in thinking through the 'why' behind the desire.

I think that the narrative behind a name change is of utmost importance; that's why I have introduced this chapter by using passages drawn from two significant interviews I conducted during my research. This chapter allows us to explore situations in which people find it necessary to change their name, whether temporarily or permanently. Further interviews and an exploration of the way that laws enable or restrict this, how some governments are strict in their naming policy and others are more relaxed, will lead us to question whether a name seems to carry less significance in some cultures, and you may find yourself reflecting on why such a change may be easier or more complex than you may imagine.

All we really want is to be known

Your name being recalled is so reassuring, just as your name being forgotten is so painful.

Expert communicators recognise this, and it can be used as a tool to edify as well as to hurt. This is because when someone calls you by your name, you feel that they care about you, that there is a form of relationship present, that they know who you are. It's an immediate sense of identity, of being seen. This can also be used as a power play. The humiliation of your name being forgotten in front of others by someone in authority or someone you thought you had built a relationship with, is crushing.

What if every time you were called by your name you felt uncomfortable, sad, or awkward because you didn't like your name? Or what if you had to lose your name?

Six years ago, a lady shared with me her desire to change her name. I was shocked and honoured as she tearfully related how she had hated her name as she grew up, feeling that it never reflected her true nature. Take a moment to consider how you would have responded if you had been in my position and why that would be the case. This is fundamental to the uniqueness of the human experience and illustrates the biggest difference between naming a thing and naming a human: vulnerability. The human has the ability to change, even reject the name given.

Much of this hinges on the nature versus nurture debate. Is your identity something that you are born with and grow into (nature) or does who you are evolve out of your experiences (nurture)? To what extent do you believe that you grow into an identity? If you believe that your identity is your own creation in response to what happens to you in life, shouldn't you, like Sean Love Combes, have the freedom to change your name to more accurately reflect who you are and are becoming as you go along?

From another angle, if we go back to a name being a way that we share or commune, then maybe one would change a name if there wasn't the agreement in what is being shared. It could be that the named never connected with the namer and so never really caught what was in their heart. It could also be that the named rejected the namer and so also wanted to reject the name.

The first person with the power to change an individual's name would be a parent. Maybe there was a rush of blood to the head in the birthing suite and the parents had completely forgotten the solemn promise made before siblings that a certain ancestor be recognised and honoured, or maybe the name chosen was just too common. This was the distressing reality for one mum who was desperate to not see history repeat itself. Writing on a 'Mumsnet' chat forum,[2] the mum shared how much she had hated being one of five girls with the same name in her class and had 'vowed never to have my [daughter] live with the same'. When it became clear that her daughter would have the same name as two other girls in her nursery, the mum was considering changing her four-year-old's name before the September start. Responses to this post ranged from, 'Are you out of your mind! She's four!' to 'Is her name Rose?' (a clever play on Shakespeare's timeless question – see chapter four). Professor Wheeler (the entomologist I interviewed for chapter three) changed his child's name legally after a week – why? Neither parent was keen on the chosen name as a first name but had thought that the other one really liked it. It was subsequently kept, but as a middle name.

To explore reasons for a name change, I've settled on five subheadings:

I choose to change FROM – This happens when there is a rejection of the name. This name you grew up with has never felt right and you have always wanted to change it.

I choose to change TO – It's not that you have always disliked your name, it's just that you are growing into someone that the name you have grown up with doesn't convey.

I am forced to change my name TO – This seems to be the most temporary of the forms; there is a sense that you must change your name in order to accomplish or realise something.

I am forced to change my name FROM – I think that this is the most painful of the categories, when an individual's name is stripped from them.

I am renamed by another – when someone you see as having a significant role in your life gives you a new name.

I choose to change FROM

In the fabulous tale *The Voyage of the Dawn Treader* (my favourite of the Narnia stories), CS Lewis introduces us to Eustace Clarence Scrubb; an individual painted as a particularly awkward and distasteful child. In fact, CS Lewis writes that the child 'deserves' the name, implying that both the name and the child are equally awful. What a fascinating line, that a boy would be given what seems to be a horrible name and have to spend his life reconciling himself to that name. As I told you at the beginning of this book, this was a journey I travelled, as have many of us. CS Lewis, it seems, had a similar road to walk. In memoirs we see that CS Lewis disliked his given Christian names: Clive Staples. It appears Eustace's name is built around the author's own name – the C (Clarence) and S (Scrubb) are there (maybe I'm overthinking it) but I wonder if there is a bit of catharsis here. Memoirs reveal that as a child, Clive took the name Jacksie from a small dog he had been fond of that had been run over and killed.[3] His change of name could quite possibly have served two functions: memorialising his feelings for the dog and also getting rid of an unappreciated given name. This went on to be shortened to Jack, which was what he was known as by family and friends.

Could it be that there is an internal battle that each of us faces when the name that we feel truly conveys who we are is not the one we are known by? I absolutely love TS Eliot's poem regarding the naming of cats in his work *Old Possum's Book of Practical Cats*. It is widely believed that cats have nine lives. However, he suggests that cats also have three names: the ones that we give them, an extraordinary name that can only ever belong to one cat, and a secret name that only the cat ever knows.

I have spoken to many people who, like me, have grown into their name. During this process you may have gone by a different name, your middle name perhaps, or a nickname. This can last a lifetime. Iconic rap artist Snoop Dogg once said: 'In the black culture, certain kids are given nicknames that they roll with forever; the nicknames outweigh their real names. I'm one of those scenarios'.[4] Even a shortened version of a name can sometimes take people by surprise at a funeral. How often do you hear about people saying, 'Well, I didn't even know that was his name!' When you hear their real name, it maybe doesn't even feel like it suits them.

Why is it that some names just don't sound right? I noticed this in the dialogue of a film I watched recently called *Extraction* featuring Chris Hemsworth. While in the middle of a rescue mission that was becoming increasingly perilous, the young character of concern turned to Chris and told him that he didn't look like a Tyler. Have you ever been introduced to someone called Kylie for example, and you've thought to yourself, or even said to them, 'That's funny, but you don't look like a Kylie! You look more like a Grace!' Maybe we build up prejudices – a mental image of what a Kylie should look like based on people you may have met or seen on TV. Maybe you grew up in the 80s and Kylie for you is synonymous with a tiny Australian girl-next-door pop sensation and you're being introduced to a tall, graceful, noble looking woman with ebony skin and entrancing eyes. Imagine growing up with this feeling about yourself, that you have been given the wrong name, or having people tell you that you have the wrong name – how confusing and unsettling! With Carmen, her estranged father changed his phone number without telling her, 'as if he'd forgotten that I existed'. This seems to have been the last straw for her: 'It felt natural to disregard his surname since he'd disregarded me. I didn't want anything that he'd given me any more'. The rejection of the scarf became much more palatable.

I choose to change TO

While researching this chapter I was struck by an Instagram post the Spanish winger Goku Roman posted. Born Joan, this instinctive goalscorer who had had a spell with Manchester City's academy amongst others, posted this:

> 'I am grateful to Joan for everything I lived, for all the positive things and lessons that name has given me, but now I am Goku. I chose this name because I feel identified with its values and what it represents to me: perseverance, empathy, growth in the face of obstacles, light and positivity. I only ask for respect regarding my decision, as many people are already doing. Always moving, always forward…'[5]

Goku is a fictional character from the Japanese media franchise *Dragon Ball* which started off in the 80s. I wonder why he felt more of a connection with this character than with what his given name represented in his eyes and in the eyes of his namer or namers. I find it fascinating that Goku saw this name as a correct reflection of his true nature and that to recognise this, or to in some way draw some sense of support in taking hold of this nature, he chose to change his name.

I wondered what people would make of this news and found this 'off-topic' conversation on a gaming forum. I love that it presents people's views to a hypothetical scenario that had just become a reality. The opening post was this:

> 'Seriously thinking of changing my name to Goku or Vegeta. It's time for the future, names should be treated like gamertags, people should start being called what they want to be called. Enough of this 1900s 'John' 'Nick', this is the future'.[6]

Responses to this post were mixed and included encouragements and ridicule, but this one was my favourite:

> 'I had a mate many years ago who changed his name to "The Dragon" when he was stuck in a huge pot bubble. Seemed like a reasonable idea at the time (well actually no it didn't), although some things I guess are a little regrettable when you look back, like getting a tattoo of your gran on your forehead. I say tread with caution'.

All of us choose names online, and we often must get creative with them because our name or our favoured option was taken four years ago. In her paper named *Internet personal naming practices*, Katarzyna Aleksiejuk says, 'On the Internet where identities are mainly constructed linguistically, names play a particularly important role as a means of constructing identities, establishing one's status and shaping relationships with other participants'.[7] This method of identification is seen through differentiation and categorisation. For instance, in a dating chat room, a 56-year-old from Irkutsk might identify himself as 'CuTeGrl8' which would lead others to assume that he was maybe a petite size 8 woman, yet on a fantasy online game he may call himself 'VladtheGladImpaler'.

Katarzyna goes on to say that in some cultures or environments 'personal names may be taboo, as being too intimate or exposing, and may be replaced in everyday communication by "common" names that serve as masks, protecting the inner, "true" self'. I remember my grave, erudite Latin teacher, formerly only addressed and imagined as 'Sir', and the sense of absurd delight when we discovered that he had a first name! The sense of normality that suddenly toppled him from a lofty position of unsearchable authority, the loss of the mystique of anonymity, was tangible. He was suddenly a human being! Katarzyna culminates with this conclusion:

'In reality, an individual's identity splits into several roles performed throughout his or her life, a phenomenon which Goffman (1959) compared to acting on a stage. This "acting" is supported by systems of addressing and referencing which provide each role with a relevant "mask". For example, Maroons (a tribe in Guyana) use various names depending on the situation: "great names" in infancy, "play names" with peers, "bad names" with joking partners, "song names" as romantic nicknames used by lovers'.

I look back over my life and recognise that I have been known as William, Will, Bill, Billy, Willy, other things that cannot be written here, and a sprinkling of positive nicknames. The main ones are all derivations of my real name and the nicknames were a tool, or as labelled by the Maroons, masks – never something that I clung onto as an expression of my identity. I felt, at times reluctantly, that my real name was a golden thread that ran through my life. The quote at the start of this chapter was taken from an interview for *Vanity Fair*.[8] He changed his name from Sean John Combs to his childhood nickname Puffy. This changed to Puff Daddy, then to P Diddy before being shortened briefly to Diddy, before returning to P Diddy. Sean John was in line with his clothing brand, and then it was Swag (for a week), then back to Puff Daddy, and most recently to Sean Love Combs. I couldn't imagine changing my name through phases of my life, particularly if the change was prescribed. Yet such is the experience of many through a significant transition, like one partner changing their surname through marriage, for example. I have had conversations with women who in later life had felt that they lost a part of their identity when they took on their husband's surname at the expense of their own; a feeling compounded by those who went through the pain of that relationship ending; the relationship web that had been built over however many years revolving around someone else's name, not least the surnames of the children.

I have a friend called Tayameaca who, as a designer, completely revolutionises traditional African materials, styles and colours in her clothing. She shared with me the story behind her name change, and it started with this dream:

> 'I'm trying to get somewhere and there was what looked like a Tube map, and the whole time I've got this person guiding me, trying to get me there. They are not physically with me, but I sense they're with me as they are communicating with me in the dream. They show me a map and they say, "This is where you're trying to get to", and it says "Tayameaca" – the way I've just spelled it – and I was like, "Oh! Yeah, that's where I'm trying to get to, but that's not the right spelling... sorry, that's not how I spell it." And they were like, "No, that is the right spelling". I was just like "OK". It was like I had an awakening, that I literally got the answer to my dream right there. So, I went into a time of praying and fasting for seven days about my name. Gradually it occurred to me that I need to change my name to that spelling. It's been five years awakening to the reality of it and getting more information and more understanding of what I need to do in stages until I finally decided "OK, I'm going to change my name to this".'

This interview reveals how Tayameaca had a sense that she was being drawn to step into something that the name represents. There was a deep, spiritual connection that Tayameaca made with this name. There was a deep call for Tayamika (the original spelling) to this name. If there isn't that, then is it surprising if its foundational status is questioned?

In the earlier interview, M's relationship with her name was less rigid. She recognised it mattered and that through it there was an honouring, but there was still a questioning. 'I just think that M is fitting for now, but I don't think that it's eternal in that sense. I'll just see how long it carries me because I feel like the name deserves me and I deserve the name, and I'm honouring it and honouring my dad's brother, my uncle.' At the time of publishing, M let me know that she considered Nicolas, the name given by her mother, as a deadname. I am keen to explore this more as I continue my research: the term 'deadname' is one that deserves addressing. I think that this concept validates some of the points made throughout this chapter, and the book as a whole.

This use of a name can be temporary as well as permanent. I have spent time with many East Asians who insist on using their Western name as described in chapter six. For them there is a sense that they are helping westerners by making things easy for us and to prove a desire to integrate and be a part. In my opinion, relationships are always both ways, a reaching out from each. So, my approach to this reaching out is to receive it in the heart it is given, but also to reach out from my side by showing an interest in their culture and history, as mentioned in the previous chapter. I recently interviewed Tom Simpson who adopted a new name 'Zhao Tang' as he moved to China in order to relate with people and connect with a new culture in a similar fashion:

> 'Usually if foreigners do choose a name, they go for something more colourful or imaginative, but there is a back story to my "Zhao". I was in the Xinjiang province 2004–05 and met Zhao Yiqun. He opened everything up and talked to us about everything that was going on and had been going on for the last 40 to 50 years. [People tried to suggest names for Tom but none of them felt right.] It didn't connect with me. Zhao was settled early on, but it took another six months or so to settle on Zhao Tang. Tang is basically my given name, Tom, which felt right because it's actually who I am, it's my identity. In Chinese it means soup and can also be a surname in certain contexts. Some people when they see my name, they think I'm Chinese because they think that I've got

two surnames put together. When they find out who I really am, then they are really interested in finding out more about my name and the background of the Zhao story, which is a wonderful way to introduce my backstory, my early engagement with China and my Chinese father figure who looked after me at the age of 18. I have other friends who have tried to find Chinese names and they've actually had three or four different names over the last 15 years because they never really connected with a particular one.'

I love how Tom's motivation was to embrace the culture he was immersing himself in. I was particularly struck by a sense of peace he experienced with this name, that the journey of its crafting was one of relationship and thought. It really reflected who he was and that he connected with it. There was an agreement.

I am forced to change my name TO

These next two subheadings explore a forced change of name, a decision that is not of your own volition.

I have been reading a book with my daughter, a 1920s copy of *Wuthering Heights* that my great aunt gave me. While preparing to get stuck into the panoramic portrayals of passionate personalities and perfectly penned power plays, I found this insightful little gem in the preface:

> 'Averse to personal publicity, we veiled our own names under those of Currer, Ellis, and Acton Bell; the ambiguous choice being dictated by a sort of conscientious scruple at assuming Christian names, positively masculine, while we did not like to declare ourselves women, because – without at the time suspecting that our mode of writing and thinking was not what is called 'feminine' – we had a vague

impression that authoresses are liable to be looked on with prejudice; we noticed how critics sometimes use for their chastisement the weapon of personality, and for their reward, a flattery, which is not true praise.'[9]

The Brontës' name change was '...dictated by a sort of conscientious scruple...'. The *Cambridge Dictionary*'s definition of a scruple suggests that the three sisters felt that going by clearly masculine names such as Charles or Edward was 'morally wrong': 'We had a vague impression that authoresses are liable to be looked on with prejudice...' These ladies, who were clearly powerful, determined and focussed enough to produce such extraordinary writing, felt that they would experience prejudice if they had used their own names. The final indignity would have been what they believed the consequences would have been had they not done this: '...for their chastisement the weapon of personality, and for their reward, a flattery, which is not true praise'. I can only assume that they meant that their character would have been in some way besmirched and any flattery would have been considered sarcastic or in ill taste.

Let's contrast two very different books. Louisa May Alcott's book *Little Women* is a wonderful narrative on life and love, which, as a woman publishing early in the American 1860s, was completely legitimate. Here are the opening lines:

> 'Christmas won't be Christmas without any presents,' grumbled Jo, lying on the rug.
>
> 'It's so dreadful to be poor!' sighed Meg, looking down at her old dress.
>
> 'I don't think it's fair for some girls to have plenty of pretty things, and other girls nothing at all,' added little Amy, with an injured sniff.
>
> 'We've got Father and Mother, and each other,' said Beth contentedly from her corner.[10]

Why Does Your Name Matter?

This, on the other hand, is the opening paragraph of AM Barnard's sensational gothic thriller, fabulously titled *Pauline's Passion and Punishment*:

> 'To and fro, like a wild creature in its cage, paced that handsome woman, with bent head, locked hands, and restless steps. Some mental storm, swift and sudden as a tempest of the tropics, had swept over her and left its marks behind.
>
> As if in anger at the beauty now proved powerless, all ornaments had been flung away, yet still it shone undimmed, and filled her with a passionate regret. A jewel glittered at her feet, leaving the lace rent to shreds on the indignant bosom that had worn it; the wreaths of hair that had crowned her with a woman's most womanly adornment fell disordered upon shoulders that gleamed the fairer for the scarlet of the pomegranate flowers clinging to the bright meshes that had imprisoned them an hour ago; and over the face, once so affluent in youthful bloom, a stern pallor had fallen like a blight, for pride was slowly conquering passion, and despair had murdered hope.'[11]

I wonder what the background was of the writers, what burned in their veins, what their perception of their world was and how they felt about themselves. Would it surprise you that they were not different writers at all, but the same person? Yes, five years before *Little Women*, Louisa May Alcott used a nom de plume for her book about Pauline. One can imagine Louisa making the same decision as the Brontës, that this piece of writing would be better received if penned by the hand of what the reader thought was a man.

Maybe you want to change your name in order to hide yourself, either temporarily or permanently, or maybe just to blend in better. A pseudonym is something that we are well aware of in many spheres of life. I have a friend who went by a pseudonym while involved in the world of modelling. As we've seen, writers use them in response to various different pressures, expectations, or biases, perceived or real, for positive or negative reasons, and with some authors, like Elena Ferrante, we may never know their true motivation.

Surely a modern-day writer like JK Rowling wouldn't have to deal with this. Or so I thought. I was shocked when, during an interview that Joanne gave with Oprah Winfrey, she shared how her publisher thought Harry Potter's young male target audience might be put off by a book written by a woman, leading her to use her initials in the pen name JK Rowling. Furthermore, Joanne later released a series of crime fiction books under the pen name Robert Galbraith.

At first glance we may feel led to believe that we are failing to escape the horrors of the past where women weren't able to represent themselves. Baileys (that rather delicious liqueur) took a stand when they 'ignited a conversation' with their 'Reclaim her name' campaign where they 're-released 25 books by authors who used a male or gender-neutral pseudonym, putting their female name on their work for the first time.'[12] E Dumbill later called this campaign into question by pointing out that, 'In a letter to James AH Murray in 1879, the writer ME Lewes wrote 'I wish always to be quoted as George Eliot'. Further on in her enlightening article, Dumbill points out:

> 'It is also important to debunk a common misconception to understand why this campaign is misguided. In George Eliot's time, women did not have to assume male pseudonyms to be published. Writers who opted to use pen names tended to choose ones that aligned with their own genders. In fact, in the 1860s and 70s men were more likely to use female pseudonyms than vice versa. William Clark Russell, for example, published several novels under the name Eliza Rhyl Davies.'[13]

Certainly, this shows us that although it is unarguable that there can be pressure put on an individual to change their name to improve their chances of being successful, this isn't always the driving force.

I am forced to change my name FROM

I had imagined that examples for this section would be those told by an individual who had to change their name due to being taken into witness protection or in order to somehow escape being found by those wanting to inflict harm in some way, for example a controlling regime.

Needless to say, volunteers weren't easy to come by to share these stories. I realised that the stories I'd heard of the Nazis stripping the Jews of their names and giving them a number was the most brutal expression of this, so I searched for an authority on the subject. This is what ultimately led me to Professor David Patterson who shared this during our interview:

> 'One of the things that distinguished the Nazi assault on the Jews, which was an assault on the soul, was to erase their names. They took away their names and put numbers on them and they had to repeat their number in German in order to get whatever ration was being passed down. I've seen interviews with survivors immediately after the war who had to make an effort to remember their name.... The name is something for us to live up to; as we recall, the soul is made out of it. I mentioned that the Nazi's assault was on the soul, which is an assault on human relationship. To bear a name is to be a light unto others.'

This removal of a name is utterly and intentionally dehumanising, and in Victor Hugo's book *Les Misérables* one of the characters, previously referred to by a number, demonstrates this as he proudly declares he is Jean Valjean in defiance and proclamation of his freedom before his captor.

I am renamed by another

To be renamed by another requires certain key elements. You must be able to trust the individual giving you this name. Do they know you well enough to have your best interests at heart, and will they support you in the transition as you take this name on? Lastly, do you have support outside of the influence of the namer? Stalking Cat (also known as 'Catman') did an interview[14] with Shannon Larratt on BME Radio several years before his death in 2012. At the age of 10, Dennis Avner had been given the name 'Stalking Cat' by Grey Cloud, the medicine man of the tribe he grew up in (Huron/Wyandot). I wonder about the significance of this man as a namer and the impact of Dennis not really knowing his father as he grew up. As he settled into adulthood the internal connection with the name started to manifest physically to an ever-greater extent. During the interview he recognised that he had been brought up with this destiny in mind by people he said knew him better than he knew himself. He went on to elaborate that the cat wasn't just his totem (companion/spirit being), but it was actually part of who he was. He shared how he relied on drink and drugs to dull the empathy and connections he felt with animals until he got progressively more in touch with his totem and ultimately 'who I really am'. Tattoos were followed by ear modifications, fillers, a lip cleft, inch long incisor teeth and the implantation of devices that enabled him to wear whiskers. Financial limitations thwarted the addition of claws and a tail.

Take a moment to consider how you would have responded if someone that you deeply respected had said to you at the age of 10 that your name was so connected to an animal. According to a lot of what I've written, Dennis did so much the right way. He really grasped this name; he looked to understand and respond to the heart of the namer, to say 'Yes'. However, it seems that the disconnect with reality that wound around the process became a noose about his neck rather than a foundation on which to stand.

Time and time again spiritual authorities clearly see names as being significant. Ancient texts record that God often inspired the names of individuals before birth, often going against cultural traditions.

Critically though, we also read that adults' names were changed – In Genesis 17 we see the change of Abram (Exulted Father) and Sarai (Princess) to Abraham (Father of Many) and Sarah (Mother of Nations). This couple are the patriarch and matriarch of Judaism, Islam and Christianity. This authority was then demonstrated again in the Bible's New Testament where a change of name reflected a shift in mandate: Simon to Peter and Saul to Paul. I love how N Pumfrey puts this:

> 'When a person is named in the narratives of Genesis, the naming attaches to that person a characteristic found throughout the story. When the original name is changed, a significant shift in the person's character occurs because the name's meaning also implies the essence of the person. In the rest of the narrative, the character will take a different role from his/her original name because the essence of the person equates with the new name. For example, when Abram cuts a covenant with YHWH, he is an exalted father. YHWH promises to make Abram a father of nations and renames Abram as Abraham; therefore, in the rest of the narrative, Abraham fulfils his name as the father of Ishmael and Isaac, whose descendants populate a nation.'[15]

I think that this highlights the amazing faith that Dennis had in Grey Cloud, that he would receive this new name with such faith that he would build his whole identity around it, in the same way that Abraham and Sarah did. However, I think that the relationship that Abraham and Sarah had would have been one that ensured faith was connected to a wholesome questioning of reality, while for Dennis there seems to have been a lack of ongoing accountability and support.

This brings me back to Plato, Homer and the ancient Greeks. There was an underlying belief that the gods knew names better than we did. Homer, in his book *The Iliad*, writes about a battle between gods. One of these battles was between Hephaestus and a river god: 'The great, deep-eddying river, that the gods called Xanthus, and men Scamander.' Plato explores this in his book *Cratylus* when he writes:

> 'He often speaks of them; notably and nobly in the places where he distinguishes the different names which gods and men give to the same things. Does he not in these passages make a remarkable statement about the correctness of names? For the gods must clearly be supposed to call things by their right and natural names; do you not think so? ... Or about the bird which, as he says, "The gods call Chalcis, and men Cymindis" to which Hermogenes replies "Why, of course they call them rightly...."'[16]

How easy should it be to change a name?

Why do some cultures resist name changing so firmly?

Rules around everything vary from country to country, particularly when they govern such controversial concepts as changing your name. This intrigued me, so I interviewed Dr Jenny Gesley from America's Law Library of Congress after coming across her blog about naming laws in Germany,[17] and this is what she told me:

> 'My colleagues wrote articles about naming laws in other countries; you probably heard about the girl in New Zealand who was named "Talula does the Hula from Hawaii", Icelandic names and others. We were talking about how easy it is to change the name depending on what the different laws are in those countries. In the US, for example, it's so easy to change your name, whereas in Germany it's so difficult. Also, personally I always find it very interesting; names are very interesting. There was another case where an Icelandic girl was fighting to keep her given name, and because her case went on for such a while she was

>just called "Girl"; I found that very interesting. [I will share research I found relating to this case later.] In Germany the resistance to changing names I think comes from this right to name a child from the Basic Law of the right of the parents to raise their child as they see fit. The Federal Constitutional Court says it is one of the foremost things that a parent can do, to name a child and give them an identity.'

One of the things I found fascinating about this interview was the way that the namer and the named have rights and responsibilities. It would be great to do a comparative study linking the individual's freedom about their rights and responsibilities with their freedom to change name.

Iceland, for example, would be considered a very free nation, with the individual's rights and responsibilities honoured and respected. However, when I interviewed Sigrún about naming practices in Iceland (the majority of which is in chapter six), she shared this about the laws in Iceland and the way in which naming is safeguarded:

>'We are very traditional, so much so that we have a committee which is called the 'Naming Committee' and meets twice a year. Its mandate is to safeguard the Icelandic naming traditions and to prevent people giving children names that were either just fashionable or could cause the child to be bullied. And after they have gone through all the names that have been submitted, both those approved and those rejected are published in the newspaper! ... The name has to have an Icelandic history, which is very controversial; a lot of people think that this is ridiculous, that this is outdated, that parents should be allowed to name their child what they want. But this is to safeguard a tradition that is over a thousand years old, which only 340,000 people live by. With the coming of the

Internet and advances in technology we seem to be losing languages, and our traditions could quite easily just disappear and be lost in history books if it's not safeguarded to an extent. There are many times where a parent has wanted to name a child something and following the refusal, they have taken the committee to court. Sometimes the court has to back down when the parents provide documentation that the name was used, say, 300 years ago.'

Isn't this a terrific insight into how the laws and practices in Iceland aren't just about protecting the individual, but the culture, identity and nature of a people group? In the interest of presenting a balanced view, here are some more details about the case that Dr Gesley referred to earlier: how an individual had to be called simply 'Girl' for an extended period of time as their birth name had initially been rejected by the Naming Committee. The plaintiffs later won the right to use the name given by her mother as the Reykjavik District Court overturned the committee's rejection. The name the committee rejected was Blaer Bjarkardottir. The BBC reported that 'Blaer's mother, Bjork Eidsdottir, has said that she had no idea that Blaer was not on the list of accepted female names when she gave it to her daughter'.[18] The article states that there are 'some 1,853 approved female names on the Icelandic Naming Committee's list'. The grounds on which the name had been rejected by the panel were that Blaer (which means 'light breeze') was too masculine a name for a girl.

I decided to follow up on Sigrún's concerns about losing languages and found an article by J Temperton. He reports: 'It is estimated that one language is driven to extinction every 14 days – and that's despite an increase in the number of languages supported by the internet.... There are currently around 7,100 languages in use, but 90 percent of these are spoken by less than 100,000 people'.[19] *Ethnologue* (a website dedicated to the languages of the world) goes into even greater depth: 'This is a fragile time: Roughly 40% of languages are now endangered, often with less than 1,000 speakers remaining. Meanwhile, just 23 languages account for more than half the world's population.'[20] What is your opinion? Are you willing to agree that in this context the desire to protect and sustain culture trumps an individual's freedom to choose a name?

It seems to me that there is a correlation between the national sense of the importance of identity, individually as well as corporately, and the ease of changing one's name. This would be a fascinating study to explore in greater depth.

***

How about you? In words taken from the deed poll website, would you be prepared to 'ABSOLUTELY and entirely renounce relinquish and abandon the use of [your] old name'?[21] Could you wholeheartedly reject this gift given by your namer, or are the reasons to change overwhelmingly compelling? I can't imagine the pain that someone would have gone through to come to a place where they believe that to fully step into the next chapter of their life requires a change to their name. But I know it happens. If you are considering changing your name out of choice, I'd like to encourage you to, if possible, reach out to your namer one last time to really try and capture what was in their heart when they gave you your name. It may not be obvious at first, even from their telling. However, be open to not only listen, but to hear. Sometimes in the asking you may unveil something that the namer hadn't even seen. If that isn't possible, if there is no way to contact them or they have died, then find someone who knew their heart. Finally, it could be that you find lines of thought and suggestions in chapter nine that may serve you well in the next step of your journey with your name.

If you think that coming to terms with your own name was challenging, then what about the pressure on the namer? In the following chapter, we're going to explore the burden placed on someone who has the responsibility to bestow a name.

8

To Give a Name

It is not how much we give, but how much love we put in the giving.

Mother Teresa[1]

How much love do you put into your giving?

The previous chapter looked at the process of changing a name, what could lead to this decision and its implications, as well as how some cultures are very open to doing this – holding the sanctity of the name and the gift of it lightly – while others resist the notion of it being something that can be rejected, changed or devalued. It's intriguing to wonder whether the greater responsibility for a name is on the giver or the receiver of that name. This chapter explores the responsibility of and the burden that giving a name puts on the namer for two reasons. Firstly, if you have been a namer this chapter will sharpen your consideration into why you gave the name you gave. Secondly, if you are to be a namer, or are to be a counsel to someone else, this chapter will give insight into why the giving is such a beautiful challenge.

Giving a name is an expression of love, and often a matter of faith, although often others don't draw on these virtues in the way the namer did. The film *A Love Song for Bobby Long* portrays a story of reconciliation and a young woman exploring her identity through retracing the steps of her past. As an adult, Pursy moves back to the area she grew up in as a child. The key scene for me is instigated when a neighbour she has no real recollection of calls her fondly by her name, Purslane. When challenged by Pursy as to who he is, he reveals that her mum involved him in naming her after the golden flower. Pursy's negative retort in response to this shows that she carries a sense of shame in her name; apparently after running through a different neighbour's vegetable patch, the neighbour spitefully told the exuberant nine-year-old that Purslane was a weed and that gardeners hate it. You could almost imagine her dream-shattering acceptance of this perspective. Suddenly this beautifully carefree child had been told that her name was linked to something that was despised and rejected, through which the speaker deliberately implied that she was as well. I reflected on how for her, and indeed many of us, the reassuring voice of the namer to override these taunts had never been there. What touched me so deeply was this man's redemptive response. He flipped the curse on its head, reminding her that as an axillary bloom, Purslane's beauty is actually hidden when it gets dark. By sharing this he was speaking life and hope into her. What if the reason she feels closed up, hidden, un-beautiful, is that she has been bound up in darkness for so long? What if when the sun starts shining again her beauty will be revealed? Even as I type this I'm moved to tears. The film follows Pursy starting to experience and fight for light in her life, and her subsequent flowering, despite others trying to keep her in the darkness of the lie. Imagine the resilience she shows when again told that a weed can only ever be a weed. In his desire to keep her bound to a form of darkness, an ex-boyfriend uses these words to undermine the very foundation of her identity through again drawing a negative association with her name. The film is littered with messages about how fragile life is, as well as the transformation that takes place when someone believes in you; how you start to dare to believe in yourself and, subsequently, others. I believe that a name can be something that you can hold onto when other aspects of life shift and change, which is why I associate the giving of a name with some trembling, some sense of awe, a drawing from and a reaching into.

The weight of naming a thing and naming a human

Earlier in this book I shared part of an interview with Professor Wheeler. I went deeper in the interview and asked him what it was like the first time he named an insect and then to try and put into words how it had felt, as well as the response of a particular individual who had been the inspiration behind the name of one of the species:

> 'I've taken a lot of heat for some of the names, particularly the political ones, but those were done intentionally just to get attention for taxonomy and the biodiversity crisis. I was living in London at the time, working at the Natural History Museum, when the paper came out naming a beetle after [President] Bush and [Dick] Cheney. My secretary called through to me and said that the White House was on the line. I thought that it would be the press office getting in touch after the name had hit the media, so I picked up the phone expecting some low-level person and I heard this voice say, 'Professor Wheeler?' I said 'Yes'. 'Please hold for the President,' and the next voice I heard was George W Bush. He spent a good five minutes talking and he actually followed up with a handwritten note as well! What a thrill that was.'

I then asked him about his own personal journey with his name, if he'd ever talked with his namer(s) as to why they bestowed this name on him, and whether or not he had always embraced his name:

> 'I wrestled with my name from a young age, but everyone I have known since my first day in college knows me as Quentin. Only my siblings call me Duane (my parents have passed). When I went to get a passport for the first time, I had to get a copy of my birth certificate. When I picked it up, I saw that I didn't have a name at all! It just said in parentheses 'Boy' and so here I had this blank slate and I seriously considered [renaming myself] Charles Darwin Wheeler – what a golden opportunity to give

yourself a different name! I went with the name that my parents had intended to give me; I felt a sense of obligation to stick with it.'

Finally, I asked him to consider whether he had experienced a difference between naming a beetle and naming his own children.

'For one thing, [naming a child] wasn't a decision on my own. Certainly, I felt more weight in the process of giving a name to a child, because they have to live with that for the rest of their lives, and that's kind of an awesome responsibility.'

Choosing a name has consequences

Throughout this research journey I have been struck by the extent to which people put thought into names. I was also staggered by the lengths authors go to in choosing names for their heroes or heroines. As I think back over the many stories that have woven together my exploration of fiction, I remember Aragorn, Bilbo, Aslan and Rincewind. I decided that the best person to explore this with would be an actor who has had to climb inside the names others have given to their characters. Stephen Campbell Moore has had a remarkable journey in life as well as on stage and screen following the auspicious achievement of winning the rare and coveted Gold Medal at the Guildhall School of Music and Drama. During our interview he shared his experiences of writers naming their characters:

'With Dickens [a name is] a description of the character, it's a deep description. It's the same with the Harry Potter books, for example Dolores Umbridge… *dolor* being sorrow and *umbrage* to take offence. It gives you the kernel of who they are so that when that name is mentioned the audience, not just the person who is playing that character, knows who they are immediately. She tries to come across as being the most pleasant and kind individual, yet all you can see is the simmering umbrage underneath her. I think that that's a very pleasurable tension, that the name is what they are.'

I asked him to share about the burden of giving himself a new name, and its repercussions:

'With the actor's union you can't have two people with the same name and [my name] was taken. I had to decide quite quickly what to do. I think that I had placed myself in a category which I felt was my root as an actor. I've got a "periodish" kind of face – what harm would a double-barrelled name do me? When I came into the profession, and I had the name I became aware very quickly how a name is received. People assume that it is your real name and they have already made a lot of decisions about you. Because you have a double-barrelled name they assume that you're a lot more posh than you are, and I remember thinking "I've created a little prison here, and it's not the prison that I necessarily wanted" because if you have a name that people associate with a certain thing, it did exactly what I wanted it to do, it put me in that bracket, but what it also did was that it excluded me from all other things.'

Reflecting on Stephen's insights proved very helpful; through the name inspiring your imagination, an author would hope you would be able to connect with the character in a certain way. The author recognises the value of weighing the name to consider the long-term implications of the name on the readers and hearers of the name: What images will it conjure up in their minds? Will it resonate with the character's behaviour/background/story arc? What an opportunity he then had to weigh the choice of name he could give himself! His later musings as to whether he had chosen well are intriguing. I wonder if you have had the opportunity to give a name, then regretted the name settled on. I find this dance fascinating. How much wrestling is enough, and would a child's life be ruined if you gave them the 'wrong' name?

The mystery of naming

Last night I was talking with a friend called John, who a couple of months ago became a father for the first time. He told me about the process of choosing a name that he had gone through. As they had looked at names and their meanings, he had been struck by how so many people's nature matched the meaning of their names. He said that he had considered how the repetitive speaking of the name over an individual would be prophetic. What was he talking about and meaning by this? He was speaking of a deeper level of understanding in regard to the impact of words and a name, that by speaking something with conviction we are calling it into being, declaring it, strengthening it.

I believe that as a namer you can come to a place where you recognise that you experienced a connection with the child that drew the name out of you, that you 'looked up at what you saw' in the child. It's this ability to 'look up at what you see' that Plato insisted sets us apart from other living things.

Anthropos is Greek for human, anthropology being the study of human behaviour, biology, culture and society. Plato, speaking as Socrates in his extraordinary work *Cratylus*, suggested that the process of naming elevates us as a species and defines what it means to be human:

> 'SOCRATES: The name anthropos, which was once a sentence, and is now a noun, appears to be a case just of this sort….
>
> HERMOGENES: What do you mean?

> SOCRATES: I mean to say that the word "man" implies that other animals never examine, or consider, or look up at what they see, but that man not only sees (opope) but considers and looks up at (or reflects on) that which he sees, and hence he alone of all animals is rightly anthropos, meaning anathron a opopen.'[2]

Allow me to clarify what Plato is saying here by talking you through some ancient Greek (NB 'man' here is not gender-specific). That man alone is called *anthropos* – ἄνθρωπος in the Greek – indicates that the other animals are not *anthropos*. In other words they do not examine, or consider, or look up at (*anathron* – ἀναθρεῖ) any of the things that they see. But man has no sooner seen – that is, ὄπωπε – than he looks up at and considers that which he has seen. So, of all the animals, man alone is rightly called man (*anthropos* – ἄνθρωπος), because he looks up at (*anathron* – ἀναθρεῖ) what he has seen (*opopen* – ὄπωπε).

In chapter three I explored the difference between us as humans naming a thing and naming another human being. In light of Plato's writings, is it possible that we are the only living thing that bears the weight of giving a name? I followed this thread and found research by Professor Vincent Janik et al, into dolphins having signature whistles that they respond to and use to relate to one another. His research finds that dolphins are the only other living things that seem to do this. The question of whether or not these could be termed 'names' remains open. I was unfortunately unable to connect with Professor Janik, but here is an abstract from one of the papers he has been involved with:

> 'Bottlenose dolphins (Tursiops truncatus) develop individually distinctive signature whistles that they use to maintain group cohesion. Unlike the development of identification signals in most other species, signature whistle development is strongly influenced by vocal learning. This learning ability is maintained throughout life, and dolphins frequently copy each other's whistles in the wild. It has been

hypothesized that signature whistles can be used as referential signals among conspecifics, because captive bottlenose dolphins can be trained to use novel, learned signals to label objects. For this labelling to occur, signature whistles would have to convey identity information independent of the caller's voice features. However, experimental proof for this hypothesis has been lacking. This study demonstrates that bottlenose dolphins extract identity information from signature whistles even after all voice features have been removed from the signal. Thus, dolphins are the only animals other than humans that have been shown to transmit identity information independent of the caller's voice or location.'[3]

So, dolphins give each other a label, but to give a name to another human in the way humans do appears unique. The giving of a name carries a weight because we know it carries consequences – we know, whether or not we articulate it, that it's a mystery: there's something about a name and the way it shapes our perception of a person that evades comprehension.

Choosing a name

Sigrún Björk Olafsdottir says, 'Your name is as significant as your fingerprint; it's the greatest gift a parent gives. Naming without depth of thought or intention is denying that child a certain right'.

In many cultures the recognition of the importance of this choice leads to the need for supernatural aid. *Aish* is a Jewish website featuring articles on the Torah, the world and lifestyle. In his article entitled 'Naming a Baby', Rabbi Shraga Simmons says that 'the Talmud tells us that parents receive one-sixtieth of prophecy when picking a name. An angel comes to the parents and whispers the Jewish name that the new baby will embody.'[4] I reflect more on this in light of another scholarly interview in chapter nine, but what happens if you're not Jewish and have no intention of seeking something outside of yourself to guide you in this way?

Making a choice

Can you make a choice of this nature without supernatural input? How do people choose a name, or anything for that matter? How would you go about choosing a car?

Are you practical? Irrespective of what the make of the car is, it just ticks the right boxes: environmental impact, cost, number of seats, size of boot.

Are you swayed by history? 'Our family always buys Honda cars; we always have and always will.'

Would you look to the future? 'I can't turn up in a Peugeot when we go to visit our family in Germany.'

Or how popular it is? 'What's the most popular family car at the moment?'

The process of elimination works well – you could take 15 cars out for a test drive and just see which one 'feels' right, or rely on serendipity – 'I was walking along with the dog and saw it parked there for sale, and I just knew it was our next car.'

People use various methods as ways of choosing a name.

History: 'The first son in every generation of our family is always called Peter.'

Looking to the future: 'We can't call her Bridgette Ursula.' 'Why not?' 'I don't want my daughter (Bridgette Ursula King) feeling awkward if she marries a guy called Mr Murray.'

Popularity/statistics: 'What's the most popular male name this year, or the most common female name on the rich list?'

Process of elimination: you and your partner may independently pick ten favourite names and then choose one.

Serendipity: 'I was sitting in the park, and I heard someone shout out, 'Jack, come and get your artichokes!' and I just knew that that had to be our son's name' (Jack, not Artichoke!).

Are these methods flippant? Fair? Irresponsible? Careless? Inspiring? However it happens, these are all methods of bringing the namer to a point where there has to be a decision, a 'yes'.

I'd like to share with you the story of a man who had all the reason in the world to find naming his son easy, but, as I keep finding in people's stories, he instead sought deeper and through looking up at (*anathron*) his son, he saw (*opopen*) something different:

'I am Eugene Greco III, and my son is Daniel Joseph – he's not Eugene Greco IV. My father was Eugene Greco Jr. Eugene is of Greek origin and its English translation is 'of noble birth'. I was called Genie as a child, and growing up in the 70s, Elton John had a song out called 'Little Genie' which was awful for me. I made an inner vow to never call my son 'Eugene' at that point, as I wouldn't want him to be bullied or for his name to be a means of making fun. I thought I'd break this tradition and do something different. [My Swedish wife and I] liked the names Daniel and Joseph; both are Bible names that worked well in Swedish as well as English. My mother at that time didn't know the reason for these names and growing up in the Italian-American honour/ shame culture, I'm sure it disappointed my dad, even though he never expressed it, as it would have been interpreted as not honouring the legacy by naming my son Eugene Greco IV. My mother did emote, and did admit that she struggled to accept it, but as it turns out, Joseph and Daniel were the very names of two brothers she had lost. Joseph had fought in WWII, and I remember his generosity as a child but knew him only as Pappy (a shortening of Giuseppe, the Italian form of Joseph) without realising his actual name. And I was very close to her other brother Daniel's children growing up. So, for her it felt like a blessing and a remembrance of the legacy of her two brothers, but I'm sure that that didn't touch my father's loss of honour. I'm sure he still felt the loss.'

I find it so interesting how Eugene looked to the past, then looked to the future and decided that even though there was an expectation on him to name his son a certain way, he was going to do what he thought was best for his child.

There are many different ways to make a choice, none of them 'better' than the other. What matters is that you come to a place of peace where you feel that you have really weighed the implications of your decision. The mystery of naming means that ultimately it comes to a point where there is an unexplainable 'Yes, this is the child's name'. There is an agreement.

What is this mystery?

So why do we have this sense of weight? Why does it feel like giving a name matters? It's because of the unexplainable mystery that touches something beyond ourselves, beyond what we see and feel in the natural. I see this framed in two ways: historically and spiritually.

I would go so far as to say that to give a name is to speak history. Giving a name impacts on history in the way that Bryan (in chapter three) described the impact of naming a mountain. I love how Havel (a Czech defender of human rights) frames history. He maintains that people have dehumanised history:

> '…as though, from age to age, history were drifting somewhere high above us in some kind of fatal superworld, as though it were taking its own course, which had nothing to do with us and was utterly impenetrable, as though history were a clever divinity that could only destroy us, cheat us, misuse us, or – at best – play jokes on us… History is not something that takes place "elsewhere"; it takes place here, we all contribute to making it'.

We saw how the Icelandic naming practices held up their history and culture; we saw how with Eugene a tradition that was handed down from generation to generation was questioned and challenged and how that had implications for earlier generations, the present generation and possibly future generations, which ties in with the baton-passing illustration in chapter five. We may say that this doesn't concern us, but the part we play in the tapestry of history does matter to each one of us.

The second frame has to do with a spiritual dimension of naming, which is recognised more readily in ancient cultures. Interviews I shared with you in chapter six illustrated ancient customs, and in his thesis titled 'Names and Power', Nicholaus Pumphrey writes this:

> 'In the Ancient Near East, the name ... contained the soul of the being that it inhabited. The meaning of the name was a binding on the object or person, and the person or object forever had to live up to the fate defined by the name.'[5]

The ancient Egyptians recognised 'Ren' as the name, a particular part of the soul. On her page *The Ancient Egyptian Soul*, Jenny Hill writes:

> 'To have a name was to have an identity. If your name was lost, you were no longer a distinct person and would cease to exist. As a result, tomb owners inscribe their names all over their tombs and texts beg visitors to say their name and so help them to flourish in the afterlife.'[6]

We will explore more about this mystery in the next chapter.

***

I hope that you took my challenge at the beginning of this chapter to heart. Have you taken time to really reflect on the *why* behind the gift of the name you gave? Do you feel more equipped if you were put in the position to give a name, or counsel someone else who was?

I'd like to encourage you to look for the right opportunity to share your naming story with the individual you named. I can assure you that it will be a gift you give, and as with all gifts, it may not be received in the way you imagine it to be, but this is the nature of giving. As we found in the last chapter, this gift can be rejected, but to love is to relinquish control. Professor Patterson put it like this when we spoke:

'When we give a name to our children, to a human being, it's a way of releasing control. Allowing them to be in control of who they are, how they answer [to their name], how they endure. I know you've had moments when you've wished you could take their place, but they have to go through their own suffering. You can be there, but you can't endure their suffering for them; as much as you want to. Their name is their name.'

9

To Be a Name

Names are a great mystery.

John Steinbeck[1]

We are surrounded by mysteries. I love watching crime dramas; the building of tensions that need to be released, questions that need to be answered, resolution.

The greatest mystery of all is identity. Who am I? Where do I come from and where am I going?

We would be wise to not ignore or diminish these questions; they are inescapable and transcend culture, age, gender and class, like a nagging itch that just *demands* to be scratched. I believe that the itch is deliberately itchy because the scratching draws us to contemplate that which is eternal. Thus, names are a doorway that invite us into an exploration of this greatest mystery. Peace with your name, peace with yourself, and peace with God are inextricably linked.

***

To what extent do you believe that you are more than your name?

In the previous chapter we recognised that giving and receiving a name isn't about the number of letters the name contains or even the logical reasoning behind its bestowal. There's a mystery to it.

What would follow if you really knew who you were, if you were in a position where your name captured and reflected the essence of an identity you were completely in sync with? The authority and confidence you walked in would not be based on anything external, like your height, weight, gender, skin colour, cultural background, or your successes or failures even. That's what we're going to explore in this last chapter: the repercussions of your acceptance of your identity, your name and the importance of relationships in coming to terms with them.

You become your name

I believe you become your name, and it reminds me of pizza. When I think back to what I said in previous chapters about whether the name Philip predisposed you to a love of horses, and about the battle that Josh Swain instigated to discover who would win the right to be the one true Josh, I thought of pizza. A pizza is a food item, yet the expression of a pizza is as limitless as the name John. You know what you're getting to an extent – a bread-like base with stuff on top – but the ingredients are endless, as are the contexts in which that pizza is eaten. If you lived in New York, you could eat a slice of margherita pizza from the same 'sidewalk vendor' every day for five years, and yet your experience of it would be different every time. There are as many variations of pizza as there are ways of being your name. We resist this because we hate the idea of being categorised and prejudged (prejudiced), but that's as narrow minded as saying pizza is pizza is pizza. This is why a key part in exploring your identity lies in the relationships that surround you and their response to you. Naming goes beyond the self and is seen in lived life experience. I illustrated in previous chapters how your name is a bridge between you, others and your namer; it's transcendental.

Havel says in his book *Disturbing the Peace*:

> '[T]he kind of hope I often think about... I understand above all as a state of mind, not a state of the world. Either we have hope within us, or we don't... Hope is not prognostication [prediction of future events]. It is an orientation of the spirit, an orientation of the heart. It transcends the world that is immediately experienced, and is anchored somewhere beyond its horizons... I feel that its deepest roots are

in the transcendental, just as the roots of human responsibility are.'[2]

There are 'transcendental roots' in our make up. Hope is one of them, as is human responsibility, which I call stewardship. You know others; they are the topics of and reasons for our greatest joy and greatest sadness – love, peace, faith. In the conversation I had with Professor Patterson, he spoke about traditional Jewish insights into names:

> 'In Jewish tradition God names us; God creates the soul by saying its name. God doesn't just say the name but in saying the name God issues a summons to come forth. So, inscribed within the name is not just our identity, but our mission. Our responsibility. What we respond to when we are called by name to the text for which we were created. In Jewish tradition, we're taught that God gives the parents a moment of prophetic insight as to what the name is. They are not trying to make up a name but figure out what is. When we no longer listen to our own name and once we no longer listen to the meaning of names, it's a symptom of a spiritual malady in our community and in our society. It has to do with names, with memory, with human relationships.... Wisdom is about understanding and realising what there is to love and what there is to fear, for these things all entail relationship. Loving, fearing, fearing for, being grateful for – these reveal relationship, and where there's relationship there's the name.
>
> The idea that we don't name ourselves is very important. The name comes from our parents, from God, or from whatever you understand as the elsewhere, because our name precedes us. Our name signifies a goodness that we don't choose but that chooses us. We are

chosen by our name. Our name is an assignment. To take away a person's name is to take away the calling, the mission, which is our identity. Whatever meaning we have lies between us, not inside of us. The soul, the *neshamah*, means breath, and the soul draws its breath from that between space. It draws its breath on the utterance of and answering to your name and calling out to another by name. To know our name is to have a capacity for hearing. The most fundamental prayer in Judaism is the Shma – to hear.

Listen. Listen carefully. We can't be the ground of our own meaning, any more than we can pick ourselves up by our own hair. It transcends us, it's from beyond us and the meaning attached to what my life means is engraved in my name.'

Recognising your name as a calling to meaning is fascinating. I also find his sense of identity being the 'between' compelling. When I started trying to piece together my thoughts on identity, my friend Rudi brought a phrase from a book called *The Religious Sense* to my attention: 'I am you who are making me'.[3] I was captivated when he first shared this with me, that my identity isn't something that I can deduce on my own, but that I am defined in and through relationships. It is an ongoing unveiling that takes place in collaboration with those around me, and ultimately with God.

If any of this is true, then those whom we allow to partner with us in the exploration of these mysteries are critical. They can be healthy and life-giving, suffocating and even destructive. Part of his road to embracing his identity involved Stalking Cat believing that those in his echo chamber were right when they encouraged his acceptance of the name and characteristics of a cat. I come to know myself through the eyes, as well as the words and actions, of those I am surrounded by. We all do this. The question is: Who walks with you, and who is in your echo chamber? To whom do you give that right? We have the power to say yes or no in our echo chamber, self-reflection, meditation and introspection – all of these are important as we have a 'response-ability' to weigh what we feel, hear and see. A further word of warning – having no one in your echo chamber is as damaging a choice as having everyone.

Echo chambers

An echo is a phenomenon whereby a sound leaves a source, hits a type of sounding board and then returns to the source. It can be unchanged or changed on its return depending on the condition of the material it makes contact with before its return. In seeking clarification on our identity, the unspoken question 'Who am I?' is answered by those we come into contact with in every walk of life. The responsibility is then to decide which echoes to listen to, to harbour, to allow to be written into our memory and onto our hearts. Do you still ask this question? In the Bible we can see how a change of echo chamber was linked to the purification of an individual's identity. It is believed that Saul's Latin name was Paul, but he had grown up as Saul (a Hebrew name which means 'to ask' or 'to question') in his Jewish surroundings. This was his echo chamber. The decisions he made in response to the echoes and responses he received led him to becoming a murderer, sanctioned by authorities. He was so well-regarded that the permission he was granted to bring those who had become Christians to Jerusalem for trial and probable execution was complete. The Bible tells us in Acts 9 how on the way to carrying out this mandate God revealed Himself to Saul. Broken and humbled, he was called to a new vision and purpose. His transformative conversion was at first distrusted by those he had previously persecuted, but as he went out to serve a new vision he used his Latin name Paul, which means 'humble'. His conversion from the pinnacle of pride to sacrifice was humbling in every way as he became the one who was vilified, imprisoned and then martyred.

Who is your sounding board, and are those you allow to respond to your deepest questions trustworthy? In the same way that the twisted and bent mirrors at a fairground can distort the original image, we can, often unknowingly, elicit a corrupt response. I love watching shows like *X Factor*, where the most stunning vocalists are given everything they need to craft and hone their vocal talent into something extraordinary. My children enjoy the outtakes which feature individuals who have been misled through unmerited praise. 'But Simon,' the contestants howl, 'give us another chance, another song… you would be mistaken to disregard us!' The tragedy is that they often simply can't sing well enough, and this man and his panel of judges are the perfect echo chamber. They were probably the first people capable of assessing the individual's voice. Who had told these individuals that they had the necessary talent to sing on a global stage? Who encouraged them into this position, resulting in such heartbreaking humiliation? Echo chambers of falsehood are environments where people are misled. Mostly it's the blind leading the blind; the tragedy is that occasionally those who can see deliberately lead others astray.

Who are you to tell me who I am?

A key question to ask yourself when considering who it is that you allow to speak into your life is this: is their heart that I serve them, or are they wanting to serve me? This distinction is critical and is the difference between control and love. Are they willing to make sacrifices for me? Do they love me unconditionally? Do they say sorry without expecting it to be reciprocated? Are these unrealistic qualities in friends, are they too high a standard? Maybe they are, but the heart attitude in trying to attain them would be evident.

We desire to know who we are, and we seek our identity through the eyes of those around us. We yearn for the words 'I see you'. One of the lines in James Horner's song for the film *Avatar* talks about seeing yourself through the eyes of the other. This insight and connection deepen as we become vulnerable before one another, and we are accepted not just for our strengths but also in an awareness of our frailties. To be accepted despite a knowledge of our mistakes and failures is love. When you love someone, you hold onto them through their storm because of who they are rather than what they have or haven't done. I wonder how damaging it is for us when words like love, faith and hope are seen as irrelevant ideals rather than fundamental human characteristics. Cherish those you have in your life who love you.

***

What is the purpose of making identity a mystery? Why risk misleading echo chambers and lives that go down unfulfilled, blind alleys? Freedom. The gift of choice. This gift of free will is extraordinary and it takes me to the other swordsmith's interview, the one I alluded to in chapter three, who asked to remain anonymous. I shared with him my reflections on the relationship between the bearer of the sword and the sword itself, and he said this:

> 'That fascinates me as a maker of swords. Sometimes I'll be making a sword, and something suggests itself to me [as a name for the sword] when I'm making it. The naming that I do is only in my head. What it does is it keeps me engaged. It keeps me within the nature of what I'm doing. I never sell a blade with a name. I give the owner of that blade that responsibility.'

I was moved by how the maker got a sense of the nature and the name of the blade as it was being formed but acted with such generosity towards its steward. Your namer was given the responsibility to name you. You are given the freedom to live as you choose. I reflected on this generosity as I remembered another story I was told of a woman who gave a child a name that was more about her own pain than about the hope she had or the future she saw for the child. When she had told her partner that she was pregnant, he rejected her. She then named the child Kurambwa, which means 'rejected' or 'not loved'. That's the name that was in the heart of the namer, but it's not necessarily the name that was in the heart of the maker. That child's identity is more than the name they've been given. I'm sure that it's rare for one of the maker's swords to be given the name he would have given, but he was willing to give that mandate away. He told me that his reasoning was this: 'In your heart you know that they're good characters and they've got a reason to own and name the sword.' This last line is so insightful: The maker puts the responsibility of naming in the hands of the individual who carries the sword, much in the same way that God, who knows your true nature and essence, gave your namer that responsibility with you. How comforting and yet sobering that those of us who play a part in bringing a child into our world are given this level of belief and trust.

Certainty of identity reflected in the grasp of your name

As we have seen throughout this book, your name is a point of connection with your identity. I remember being struck as I read an account of the impact a particular individual had on those who listened to Him. This individual had absolute certainty and acceptance of His name and how it connected with His identity:

> 'Judas then, having received the Roman cohort and officers from the chief priests and the Pharisees, came there with lanterns and torches and weapons. So Jesus, knowing all the things that were coming upon Him, went forth and said to them, "Whom do you seek?" They answered Him, "Jesus the Nazarene." He said to them, "I am He." ... So, when He said to them, "I am He," they drew back and fell to the ground' (John 18:3–6 NASB).

What an extraordinary event! The force of the declaration, this certainty of identity, was enough to knock people over, possibly including Roman soldiers. Jesus had surrounded Himself with teachers, had sought to understand who He was in light of scripture and had wrestled with God in the face of His calling. He knew who He was.

Right at the beginning I mentioned *gravitas*, the weight of something or someone. I am often surprised at the way people use the words 'I am'. In one of my YouTube videos I refer to a scene in a Marvel film where a character says 'I am Ironman' as an explanation of his identity and the justification behind his actions. I'd like you to give this a try. Instead of (for example) saying 'My name is Adil' the next time you introduce yourself, try 'I am Adil'. Even running the scenario through in your mind will cause you to reflect on what I've written in a new way. Oh, and don't cheat and shorten it to 'I'm Adil' – there has to be an intentionality behind it, as though by saying your name you are saying something significant. Try practising in the mirror.

I believe that even a woman whose name is 'Unloved' can be reconciled to her name. Getting back to her namer and exploring the heart behind the name could be key, as there is always hope. It could be that reflecting on the name could bring healing to the namer which could lead to a renaming or a resolute adoption that would define their story: 'I was named Unloved because of this and this, but I know that I am actually loved and my name doesn't really reflect what I know to be true'. The search for a restoration of relationships is something that is beyond your control. You may reach out, but there may be no one to find, or the answer to the call may be one of rejection. Regardless, please try. Even so, you may still come to the point where the only answer is to change your name, as the lady who came to me did. You have to strengthen your ability to say and hear your name.

***

'[There needs to be] … a recovery of a capacity for being able to hear your name. Our names are being called out by people around us in all kinds of ways. People who need a helping hand, a good word, sometimes without them maybe saying anything. The look in the eyes. Years ago, when I was walking in Paris, I came across a young woman who was begging on the sidewalk. She had her face buried in one arm and had her hand stretched out, she didn't speak a word. I shuddered at the sight of her, and I heard my name being called by her silent, outstretched hand. People are reaching out to us in all kinds of ways.

For me personally, in the human hand reaching out, God is reaching out. It's the original question: [found in Genesis following Adam and Eve's eating of the fruit, God calls out] "Where are you?" If you don't know your name, you can't say "Here I am".' (Dr David Patterson)

Everything we have explored and wrestled with in this book leads us through progressively deeper engagements with identity. For example:

I recognise that words and names matter.

I recognise that names have meaning.

I like the name Fiona.

We take a deeper step – what does Fiona mean? I may use Wikipedia to discover its meaning as 'fair/white/vine'[4].

We take a deeper step – 'What was in the heart of your namer?' It may be that Fiona was the name of a person who was kind and caring to your namer as they grew up. This insight could lead to reconciliation with your namer.

We take a deeper step – 'What was in the heart of your maker?' This step can lead you to reconciliation with God.

If there is no 'Yes' in your heart because you don't relate to your name – if you have no idea of what it represented in the heart of your namer or you have rejected the namer and the name – then I would urge you to seek out the heart of your maker, who knows you, loves you and sees you completely.

We try to demonstrate this integrity when as parents we hold on to what we believe of our children when others say how awful they are. We understand discipline and the importance of just consequences for behaviour, but crucially we know the difference between who they are and the mistakes that they make. In the same way that the swordsmith did, there was a knowing of you before a breath was taken. How can I be sure of this? Because knowing the one who can say 'I AM WHO I AM' has brought me healing and hope. This relationship, through Jesus, has been and will be an anchor through my storms of brokenness while also strengthening my resolve as I press on to truly live. Furthermore, it is what people experience when they use me as part of their echo chamber. One of the key passages from the Bible in this journey is from Psalm 139 (NASB):

'For You [God] created my innermost parts; You wove me in my mother's womb. I will give thanks to You, because I am awesomely and wonderfully made; wonderful are Your works, and my soul knows it very well. My frame was not hidden from You when I was made in secret, and skilfully formed in the depths of the earth.'

***

You are known, you were created, you are loved. This relationship with God is not based on what I do, or how closely I stick to a set of rules or regulations. It's a relationship that started before I was born and is continually unveiled as I reach into it through the turmoil, the confusions and the celebrations of life. I'd like to invite you to restore this relationship too – because in so doing, you will come to know not only your maker, but your own true nature as well. Jesus is the way to this relationship. The Bible tells us that the name of Jesus brings freedom, healing and forgiveness, that it is above every other name. My dear brother Riaan said, 'There's no name on earth like the name of Jesus. If you have ever experienced the power vested in this name, you won't be able to ever keep quiet.'

***

I believe that your willingness to explore and wrestle with these mysteries, to grapple with every clue and turn every key, is in direct proportion to the extent to which you will come to terms with who you are and why you are.

REFERENCES

Introduction

1. 'Reconcile', *Online Etymology Dictionary*, https://www.etymonline.com/word/reconcile, accessed 11 Feb 2020.
2. 'Onomastics', *Dictionary.com*, https://www.dictionary.com/browse/onomastics, accessed 18 Sep 2019.

1 Knowing Me

1. Emerson, Ralph Waldo, 'The Divinity School Address', 15 Jul 1838, Harvard University, Cambridge.
2. 'Introduction', *Online Etymology Dictionary*, https://www.etymonline.com/search?q=introduction, accessed 15 Jul 2021.
3. 'Identity', *Online Etymology Dictionary*, https://www.etymonline.com/search?q=identity, accessed 4 May 2020.
4. Herrmann, M, 'The Return of the Pie Company That Gave the Frisbee Its Name', Atlas Obscura (2019), https://www.atlasobscura.com/articles/frisbee-history, accessed 20 Oct 2021.
5. Thoreau, HD, *Walden*, (20th edition, London: Arcturus, 2020).
6. Ducharme, J, 'Why You Forget Names Immediately–And How to Remember Them', *Time* (2018), https://time.com/5348486/why-do-you-forget-names/, accessed 5 Dec 2021.
7. Turner, J, *Philology: The Forgotten Origins of the Modern Humanities* (Princeton: Princeton University Press, 2015), 3.

2 Knowing You

1. Byron, George Gordon, *Don Juan* (Oxford: Oxford University Press, 2008).
2. 'Communicate', *Online Etymology Dictionary*, https://www.etymonline.com/search?q=communicate, accessed 11 Dec 2019.
3. Leys, Simon, *The Analects of Confucius* (New York: WW Norton & Company, 1998), 181.
4. 'Why Is Confucius Still Relevant Today? His Sound Bites Hold Up', National Geographic (2015), https://www.nationalgeographic.com/news/2015/03/150325-confucius-china-asia-philosophy-communist-party-ngbooktalk/, accessed 22 Sep 2020.
5. Qiao, L and Min, S, 'A Study on Confucius' Views on Language Functions', *Polyglossia* 16 (Feb 2009). doi: 10.34382/00011665
6. 'Philology', *Online Etymology Dictionary*, https://www.etymonline.com/word/philology, accessed 11 Dec 2019.
7. Telephone conversation with the author, 11 Jun 2020
8. Shlain, L, *The Alphabet Versus the Goddess: The Conflict Between Word and Image* (London: Penguin, 1999).
9. Darnell, JC, Dobbs-Allsopp, FW, Lundberg, MJ, McCarter, PK, Zuckerman, B, Manassa, C, 'Two early alphabetic inscriptions from the Wadi el-Hôl: New evidence for the origin of the alphabet from the western desert of Egypt', The Annual of The American Schools of Oriental Research, 59, (Boston, MA: American Schools of Oriental Research, 2005).
10. Black, JA, Cunningham, G, Ebeling, J, Flückiger-Hawker, E, Robson, E, Taylor, J, and Zólyomi, G, 'Enmerkar and the Lord of Aratta', *The Electronic Text Corpus of Sumerian Literature,* http://etcsl.orinst.ox.ac.uk/ (Oxford: University of Oxford, 1998–2006).
11. 'Bereishith – Genesis – Chapter 10', *Chabad.org*, https://www.chabad.org/library/bible_cdo/aid/8174/jewish/Chapter-10.htm, accessed 24 Mar 2020.
12. Plato, *Cratylus*, trans Jowett, B, Project Gutenberg e-book #1616 (26 Sep 2008, updated 15 Jan 2013), https://www.gutenberg.org/ebooks/1616.

3 Knowing Things

1. Gillespie, John, 'Les Mots: Sartre and the language of belief', *Sartre Studies International* 11/1–2 (Jun–Dec 2005), 234–48. http://www.jstor.org/stable/23512971.
2. Puzey, G, and Kostanski, L, *Names and Naming* (Bristol: Multilingual Matters, 2016), xxii.
3. Telephone conversation with the author, 07 Jul 2020
4. Mortimer, P, and Bunker, M, *The Sword in Anglo-Saxon England from the 5th to 7th century* (Ely: Anglo-Saxon Books, 2018).
5. Carlin, G, *Brain Droppings* (New York: Hachette, 1998).
6. 'Why do we name tropical storms and hurricanes?', *National Ocean Service*, https://oceanservice.noaa.gov/facts/storm-names.html, accessed 17 May 2020.
7. Ainge Roy, Eleanor, 'Lusius malfoyi wasp: New Zealand insect named after Harry Potter villain', *The Guardian* (10 Oct 2017), https://www.theguardian.com/environment/2017/oct/10/lusius-malfoyi-wasp-new-zealand-insect-named-after-harry-potter-villain, accessed 25 Feb 2020.

4 To Research a Name

1. Geldof, Peaches, cited by Smith, Hortense, 'Celebrity Baby Names: Creativity Or A Curse?' *Jezelbel*, 22 Nov 2008. https://jezebel.com/celebrity-baby-names-creativity-or-a-curse-5096789.
2. Shakespeare, William. *Romeo and Juliet,* in Blakemore Evans, G, et al *The Riverside Shakespeare*, vol 2, (Boston : Houghton Mifflin, 1974).
3. Wade, IO, 'Voltaire's Name', PMLA, 44/2 (1929), 546–64. doi: 10.2307/457480
4. 'The altercation Voltaire – Rohan', *Wikipedia France*, https://fr.wikipedia.org/wiki/Altercation_Voltaire-Rohan, accessed 13 Sep 2020.
5. 'Martin Short – Biography', *Hello!* (8 Oct 2009), https://www.hellomagazine.com/profiles/martin-short/, accessed 14 Sep 2020.
6. 'Short'*, Dictionary of American Family Names* (Oxford: Oxford University Press, 2013), https://www.oxfordreference.com/view/10.1093/acref/9780195081374.001.0001/acref-9780195081374-e-57671?rskey=3Sr9lB&result=57670, accessed 14 Sep 2020.

7   'Surnames', *ScotlandsPeople*, https://www.scotlandspeople.gov.uk/research-guides/surnames, accessed 13 Sep 2020.
8   Wee, Kek Koon, 'The complex origins of Chinese names demystified', *South China Morning Post* (18 Nov 2016), https://www.scmp.com/magazines/post-magazine/long-reads/article/2046955/complex-origins-chinese-names-demystified, accessed 16 Sep 2020.
9   Bush, SJ, Powell-Smith, A and Freeman, TC, *Network analysis of the social and demographic influences on name choice within the UK (1838–2016)* PLoS ONE 13/10, e0205759. doi: 10.1371/journal.pone.0205759, accessed 14 Sep 2020.
10 Galbi, DA, 'Long-Term Trends in Personal Given Name Frequencies in the UK', *arXiv* (2002), https://arxiv.org/ftp/physics/papers/0511/0511021.pdf, accessed 16 Sep 2020.
11 Mommsen, T, *The History of Rome*, vol 1 (Oxford: Benediction Classics, 2011), 26.
12 Kessler, DA, Maruvka, YE, Ouren, J, and Shnerb, NM, 'You Name It – How Memory and Delay Govern First Name Dynamics', PLoS ONE 7/6, e38790. (2012). doi: 10.1371/journal.pone.0038790, accessed 16 Sep 2020.
13 'Popular baby names', *Social Security Administration*, https://www.ssa.gov/oact/babynames/, accessed 14 Sep 2020.
14 BBC News, *Racism in Football – Our Stories*, BBC iPlayer (Oct 2020) https://www.bbc.co.uk/iplayer/episode/m000n9g5/racism-in-football-our-stories, accessed 3 Feb 2021.
15 'Seriously thinking of changing my name to Goku or Vegeta, too crazy?', *Gamespot* (2011), https://www.gamespot.com/forums/offtopic-discussion-314159273/seriously-thinking-of-changing-my-name-to-goku-or--28957666/, accessed 14 Sep 2020.
16 Jevitt, SD and Dubner, SJ, *Freakonomics* (London: Penguin, 2006).
17 'Forbes World's Billionaires List', *Forbes* (2020), https://www.forbes.com/sites/angelauyeung/2020/04/07/with-more-billionaires-than-most-countries-californias-richest-attempt-to-step-up-to-fight-the-coronavirus/?sh=4843cdc33c49, accessed 20 Oct 2020.
18 Mehrabian, A, *The Name Game: The Decision That Lasts a Lifetime* (London: Penguin, 1992).
19 Boyce, Tessa, '25 Baby Names That Spell Career Success', *Business 2 Community* (15 Nov 2015), https://www.business2community.com/social-buzz/25-baby-names-that-spell-career-success-01375026, accessed 20 Oct 2020.

20 Wolfers, Justin, 'Fewer Women Run Big Companies Than Men Named John', *The New York Times* (2 Mar 2015), https://www.nytimes.com/2015/03/03/upshot/fewer-women-run-big-companies-than-men-named-john.html?_r=0, accessed 21 Oct 2020.
21 Montgomery, LM, *Anne of Avonlea*. (Boston: LC Page & Company, 1909).
22 Perrie, S, 'Teachers And Parents Reveal Kids' Names Linked with Best And Worst Behaviour', *LADbible* (Oct 2019), https://www.ladbible.com/community/interesting-teachers-reveal-names-of-the-naughtiest-and-best-behaved-kids-20191028, accessed 19 Oct 2020.
23 Jennings-Edquist, Grace, 'Why parents are choosing 'masculine' names for their baby girls', *ABC* (23 Jan 2019), https://www.abc.net.au/everyday/why-parents-are-giving-their-girls-masculine-boy-names/10717012, accessed 3 Jan 2021.
24 Coffey, B, Walker, J, and McLaughlin, PA, 'Do Masculine Names Help Female Lawyers Become Judges? Evidence from South Carolina', *American Law and Economics Review*, 11/1 (Spring 2009).
25 Juneau, Jen and McNiece, Mia, 'Blake Lively Sets the Record Straight on Her Daughter's Name', *People* (18 May 2018), https://people.com/parents/blake-lively-daughter-inez-correct-name-spelling/, accessed 20 Oct 2020.
26 Riach, P and Rich, J, 'An Experimental Investigation of Sexual Discrimination in Hiring in the English Labor Market', *The BE Journal of Economic Analysis & Policy*, 6/2 (2006). doi: 10.2202/1538-0637.1416
27 Smith, F, Tabak, F, Showail, S, McLean Parks, J and Kleist, J, 'The Name Game: Employability Evaluations of Prototypical Applicants with Stereotypical Feminine and Masculine First Names', *Sex Roles* 52, 63–82 (2005). doi: 10.1007/s11199-005-1194-7
28 Zweigenhaft, RL, 'The Other Side of Unusual First Names', *The Journal of Social Psychology* 103/2, 291–302 (1977). doi: 10.1080/00224545.1977.9713328

5 To Receive a Name

1 Tillich, Paul, *The Eternal Now* (Canterbury: SCM Press, 2002), 13.
2 Patterson, D, *Open Wounds, The Crisis of Jewish Thought in the Aftermath of the Holocaust* (Seattle: University of Washington Press, 2006) 104.

3. Kaneda, Toshiko and Haub, Carl, 'How Many People Have Ever Lived on Earth', *Population Reference Bureau* (18 May 2021), https://www.prb.org/articles/how-many-people-have-ever-lived-on-earth, accessed 2 Jul 2021.
4. Bartz, J, Tchalova, K and Fenerci, C, 'Reminders of Social Connection Can Attenuate Anthropomorphism: A Replication and Extension of Epley, Akalis, Waytz, and Cacioppo (2008)' *Psychological Science* 27/12 (Oct 2016). doi.org/10.1177/095679761666851
5. Aristotle, *The Politics*, trans Barker, Earnest, rev Stalley, RF (Oxford: Oxford University Press, 2009).
6. 'Mindfulness', *Wikipedia*, https://en.wikipedia.org/wiki/Mindfulness, accessed 23 Nov 2020.
7. Davis, S, *Jim Morrison: Life, Death, Legend* (London: Ebury, 2005), 409.
8. Bin Ashath, Abu Dawud Sulaiman, Sunan Abu Dawud, trans Yasir Qadhi, Y (Riyadh: Darussalam, 2008).
9. Borger, Julian, 'Meet the Kosovan Albanians who named their sons after Tony Blair', *The Guardian* (20 Jun 2014), https://www.theguardian.com/politics/2014/jun/20/kosovan-albanians-name-children-tony-blair-tonibler, accessed 14 Oct 2020.
10. Jan, 'Ruud Krol: Royalty in Naples', *Bleed Orange* (8 Apr 2017), https://dutchsoccersite.org/ruud-krol-royalty-in-naples/, accessed 8 Feb 2021.

6 To Receive Another

1. Hilton, Paris, *Confessions of an Heiress: A Tongue-In-Chic Peek Behind the Pose* (London: Simon & Schuster, 2005).
2. 'Culture', *Cambridge Dictionary*, https://dictionary.cambridge.org/dictionary/english/culture, accessed 22 Oct 2020.
3. 'Culture', *Online Etymology Dictionary*, https://www.etymonline.com/search?q=culture, accessed 22 Oct 2020.
4. 'Mahnaz Afkhami Reflects on Working Toward Peace' (2014), *Markkula Centre for Applied Ethics*, https://www.scu.edu/mcae/architects-of-peace/Afkhami/essay.html, accessed 13 May 2020.
5. 'Why should I learn a language?' *Omniglot*, https://omniglot.com/language/why.htm, accessed 31 Oct 2020.

Introduction to Part Three

1. Frank, T, 'How to remember people's names' [video], YouTube (uploaded 29 Oct 2019), https://www.youtube.com/watch?v=hkjKNrMvBlw&t=43s, accessed 11 Nov 2021.
2. 'Arbitrary', *Dictionary.com*, https://www.dictionary.com/browse/arbitrary, accessed 11 Nov 2021.
3. Pietrangelo, Ann, 'What the Baader-Meinhof Phenomenon Is and Why You May See It Again… and Again', *Healthline* (17 Dec 2019), https://www.healthline.com/health/baader-meinhof-phenomenon, accessed 12 Nov 2021.

7 To Change a Name

1. Combs, Sean, cited in McMillan Cottom, T, '"I Got a Second Chance": From Puff Daddy to Diddy to Love', *Vanity Fair* (Aug 2021), https://www.vanityfair.com/style/2021/08/from-puff-daddy-to-diddy-to-love, accessed 8 Feb 2022.
2. 'To change their name!', *Mumsnet*, https://www.mumsnet.com/Talk/am_i_being_unreasonable/3304912-to-change-their-name, accessed 1 Mar 2021.
3. Lewis, WH, 'Memoir of C.S. Lewis', *Letters of C. S. Lewis* (New York: Harcourt, Brace & World, 1966), in Gresham, Douglas, *Jack's Life: The Life Story of C. S. Lewis* (Nashville: Broadman & Holman, 2005).
4. 'Snoop Dogg Quotes', *IMDb*, https://m.imdb.com/name/nm0004879/quotes, accessed 11 Dec 2021.
5. 'Now I am Goku', *Goal* (12 Oct 2020), https://www.goal.com/en/news/now-i-am-goku-former-man-city-and-barcelona-b-star-announces/w5anz4fcbzie1736brxf63cuh, accessed 14 Oct 2020.
6. 'Seriously thinking of changing my name to Goku or Vegeta, too crazy?', *Gamespot* (2011), https://www.gamespot.com/forums/offtopic-discussion-314159273/seriously-thinking-of-changing-my-name-to-goku-or--28957666/, accessed 14 Sep 2020.
7. Aleksiejuk, K, 'Internet Personal Naming Practices and Trends in Scholarly Approaches' in *Names and Naming*, Puzey, G and Kostanski, L (Bristol: Multilingual Matters, 2016), 3–18.

8. McMillan Cottom, T, 'With love, Sean Combs', *Vanity Fair* (Sep 2021), https://archive.vanityfair.com/article/2021/9/with-love-sean-combs, accessed 23 Nov 2021.
9. Bell, C, 'Biographical notice of Ellis and Acton Bell' in Brontë, E, *Wuthering Heights* (London: John Murray), xlv.
10. Alcott, LM, *Little Women* (New York: Signet Classics, 2004).
11. Barnard, AM, *Pauline's Passion and Punishment* (London: Dodo Press, 2006).
12. 'Reclaim her name campaign', *Baileys*, https://www.baileys.com/en-gb/reclaim-her-name-campaign, accessed 1 Nov 2020.
13. Dumbill, Eleanor, 'Why it's not empowering to abandon the male pseudonyms used by female writers', *The Conversation* (Aug 2020), https://theconversation.com/why-its-not-empowering-to-abandon-the-male-pseudonyms-used-by-female-writers-144607, accessed 1 Nov 2020.
14. BME Radio, Interview between Stalking Cat and Shannon Larratt, http://www.zentastic.com/bmeradio/Cat.mp3, accessed 10 Nov 2020.
15. Pumphrey, NB, 'Names and Power: The concept of secret names in the Ancient Near East', MA Thesis, Vanderbilt University, Nashville, 2009. https://etd.library.vanderbilt.edu/etd-03272009-190249.
16. Plato, *Cratylus*, trans Jowett, B, Project Gutenberg e-book #1616 (26 Sep 2008, updated 15 Jan 2013), https://www.gutenberg.org/ebooks/1616.
17. Gesley, Jenny, 'Naming Laws in Germany' *Library of Congress Blogs* (Aug 2017), https://blogs.loc.gov/law/2017/08/naming-laws-in-germany/, accessed 20 Aug 2020.
18. BBC News, 'Icelandic girl Blaer wins right to use given name' (31 Jan 2013), https://www.bbc.co.uk/news/world-europe-21280101, accessed 20th Aug 2020.
19. Temperton, J, 'Languages are dying, but is the internet to blame?' *Wired* (Sep 2015), https://www.wired.co.uk/article/linguistic-diversity-online, accessed 8 Feb 2021.
20. Eberhard, DM, Simons, GF, and Fennig, CD (eds) *Ethnologue: Languages of the World*, 25th edition (Dallas: SIL International, 2022), https://www.ethnologue.com/guides/how-many-languages, accessed 20 Oct 2022.
21. 'Change your name by deed poll', *GOV.UK*, https://www.gov.uk/change-name-deed-poll/enrol-a-deed-poll-with-the-courts, accessed 20 Aug 2020.

8 To Give a Name

1. Mother Teresa, ed Kolodiejchuk, Brian, *Where There is Love, There is God* (London: Crown, 2010).
2. Plato, *Cratylus*, trans Jowett, B, Project Gutenberg e-book #1616 (26 Sep 2008, updated 15 Jan 2013), https://www.gutenberg.org/ebooks/1616.
3. Janik, VM, Sayigh, LS, and Wells, RS, 'Signature whistle shape conveys identity information to bottlenose dolphins', *Proceedings of the National Academy of Sciences of the United States of America* 103 (May 2006). doi: 10.1073/pnas.0509918103
4. Simmons, Shraga, 'Naming a Baby', *Aish*, https://www.aish.com/jl/l/b/48961326.html, accessed 9 Sep 2021.
5. Havel, V, *Disturbing the Peace: A Conversation With Karel Hvizdala*, trans Wilson, P (New York: Vintage, 1990) 180.
6. Pumphrey, NB, 'Names and Power: The concept of secret names in the Ancient Near East', MA Thesis, Vanderbilt University, Nashville, 2009. https://etd.library.vanderbilt.edu/etd-03272009-190249.
7. Hill, Jenny, 'The Ancient Egyptian Soul', *Ancient Egypt Online* (2017), https://ancientegyptonline.co.uk/soul/, accessed 7 Sep 2021.

9 To *Be* a Name

1. Steinbeck, John, *East of Eden* (London: Penguin, 2002).
2. Havel, V, *Disturbing the Peace: A Conversation With Karel Hvizdala*, trans Wilson, P (New York: Vintage, 1990).
3. Giussani, L and Zucchi, JE, *The Religious Sense* (Buffalo: McGill-Queen's University Press, 1997).
4. 'Fiona', *Wikipedia*, https://en.wikipedia.org/wiki/Fiona, accessed 11 Nov 2021.

Ingram Content Group UK Ltd.
Milton Keynes UK
UKHW042158250723
425784UK00012B/143/J